GORDON RAMSAY

GORDON RAMSAY

THE BIOGRAPHY

NEIL SIMPSON

JOHN BLAKE

Published by John Blake Publishing Ltd,
3, Bramber Court, 2 Bramber Road,
London W14 9PB, England

www.blake.co.uk

First published in hardback in 2006

ISBN 1 84454 218 1

British Library Cataloguing-in-Publication Data:

A catalogue record for this book is available from the British Library.

Design by www.envydesign.co.uk

Printed and bound in Great Britain by William Clowes Ltd, Beccles, Suffolk

3 5 7 9 10 8 6 4

CONTENTS

ONE

THE FIRST ****ING NIGHTMARE

'You're a total ****wit. A complete and utter ****er and you are seriously ****ing me off.'

Four production staff in the television company's editing suite sat and stared at the bank of screens in front of them in shocked silence. They had never been able to broadcast this much bad language before and no one thought that they would be allowed to start now. 'Reel it along a bit so we can check the next part,' said the producer finally. Maybe this had just been a one-off outburst that could be edited down before the show was aired.

'Your service is crap and the food itself is a fucking disgrace. You should be fucking ashamed of yourself.'

'Reel it on a bit more.'

'Fuck off. I don't want to discuss it any more. If I had my way, I'd fucking fire you on the spot and you'd never work in a fucking restaurant again if you live to be a fucking hundred.' Gordon Ramsay stormed out of view and the screen went black. There was another long, shocked silence from the production team. As one-off outbursts go, this one was taking a long time to run its course.

'Could we maybe beep it all out?' asked the researcher hopefully.

The group sat in silence once more as the sound technician did the work and then clicked on 'play'. The angry blond-haired man on screen was back and his mood didn't seem to have improved. '*Beep* hell. If you *beep* dare send food out in that kind of *beep* condition you deserve to be *beep* shot. I can't *beep* believe this. *Beep*, *beep* hell.'

'It's not going to work, is it?' said one of the production managers as the meeting ended. 'All he does is swear, so if we lose the swearing we lose the whole show. Maybe we've just got to run with it. How bad can it be? With a bit of luck, no one's going to notice.'

But, as it turned out, everyone did notice on Tuesday, 27 April 2004 when the first episode of *Ramsay's Kitchen Nightmares* was broadcast to more than four million viewers on Channel 4. When they had done the sums, television critics said Gordon had used the f-word every ten seconds at the start of the programme and ended up swearing a staggering 111 times in the 50-minute show. That more than doubled the previous British record for bad language, which had been set with the screening of the gangster movie *Goodfellas* in 2001.

'Ramsay swears five or six times a minute, uses "fuck" as a noun, an adjective and a verb, sometimes all in the same sentence, sometimes twice. It is a joy to watch,' said the normally disapproving *Times*. 'Gordon is a natural on television because he is so compelling, so passionate and so unbelievably rude,' said Lucy Cavendish of London's *Evening Standard*.

Over the next couple of days, every paper would scream out its own opinions about Gordon's unprecedented spate of bad language. Some hailed Gordon as a straight-talking hero and a true voice of the people. Others said he was going to be responsible for the end of civilised society as we knew it. Everyone, it seemed, had an opinion and Gordon refused to apologise to any of them.

'You brought the catering industry into disrepute,' said one critic immediately after the first show was aired.

'Bullshit,' replied Gordon.

'You bullied and humiliated a hapless 21-year-old chef,' said another.

'Bollocks. I didn't humiliate him. He made a fucking tosser of himself without any help from me.'

Taking part in *Ramsay's Kitchen Nightmares* in 2004 had been a huge gamble for 37-year-old Gordon Ramsay. When the producers first approached him about the show, he was one of the most successful and respected restaurateurs in the country. He employed more than 850 people, had millions in the bank and had won more Michelin stars in less time than any British chef in history. His name was above the door in some of the country's most prestigious five-star hotels, with Ramsay restaurants at the Berkeley, Claridge's, the Connaught and the Savoy.

So would taking part in a reality-television show boost his reputation as he tried to take the Ramsay brand global and open restaurants everywhere from New York and Las Vegas to Dubai and Singapore? Or would it ruin everything if he was dismissed as a foul-mouthed bully who cared more about fame than food?

Gordon says he agreed to do the show because he genuinely thought he could make a difference to the restaurants being featured. And he was determined to stop the programme being seen as a vanity television project with him as a figurehead presenter and everyone else doing all the work. 'I wanted to be physical and from the start I told the producers I didn't just want to be some bloke in a suit holding a clipboard. I went into those establishments hands-on at a thousand miles an hour and grafted because I wanted it to be a one-man crusade to turn those places around. What was unfolding at a lot of the restaurants was a worst-case scenario and we couldn't have changed it if I'd only been there for one hour a day to show off for the cameras. I was serious about putting the hours in here and serious about turning these places around.'

On a broader level, Gordon also thought he could do everyone a favour by getting involved in this extreme makeover project. 'There are too many bad places to eat in Britain when there doesn't need to be any of them,' he said. 'I've suffered and I've learned every day in my career and I think I've got enough knowledge to pass on to other people. Whether they take my advice or not is up to them. But I think I can prove I know what works.'

The first restaurant in the series would put that confidence to its sternest test – and cement Gordon's reputation as the hard man of British catering. It had been in the winter of 2003 that Gordon had first travelled up to Silsden in West Yorkshire to meet the owner and staff of the desperately troubled Bonaparte's restaurant. The man who had invited him there, 21-year-old head chef Tim Gray, had seen an advertisement in a catering magazine asking failing restaurants to get in touch if they wanted help in turning their fortunes around. And very few restaurants could live up to the word 'failing' as convincingly as Bonaparte's.

A few early statistics showed up the scale of the challenge. Owner Sue Ray had worked out that she needed to make around £2,000 a week just to cover her costs. But when Gordon arrived, she was collecting less than £200. The basement restaurant could comfortably seat 50 diners. But most nights they were serving no more than five. Sue's bankers were getting twitchy and her staff were getting worried. Tim, in particular, thought his dreams of becoming a television chef and running his own chain of restaurants would be dashed if Bonaparte's went under. The Ramsay touch was required.

The thinking behind the new show was simple. Originally due to be called *Cutting the Mustard*, it was to feature Gordon arriving at and assessing a variety of different struggling restaurants. Over up to two weeks of daily work and filming, he would try to show the staff how to raise their game and turn things around. They would then be left to their own devices for a month before he and the film crew would return to see if the transformation had worked. The idea was to be reality television with a difference. Gordon wanted to be constructive rather than destructive, and to be compared to *Troubleshooter*'s quietly spoken Sir John Harvey-Jones rather than *Pop Idol*'s famously angry Simon Cowell.

Unfortunately, his first impressions of Bonaparte's head

chef left no room for Sir John's calm reasoning. 'Ramsay does not merely eat Tim alive, he tenderises him with a mallet and then spatchcocks him,' wrote the food editor of *The Times* after watching a preview tape of the show.

The problems began when Gordon had to persuade Sue to offer free meals to diners just to get enough people into the restaurant so that he could see what £300-a-week chef Tim was capable of. It wasn't a lot.

'I see myself as cooking fine cuisine,' Tim claimed unconvincingly.

'Bollocks,' Gordon responded. 'Cook me an omelette so I can see how you do the basics.'

But Tim didn't know where to start. And when he put his strange, egg-based creation in the oven instead of on the hob, Gordon called a halt. Which was when the real television drama began.

Tim was given free rein to create his 'signature dish' in an attempt to impress his new mentor and repair his reputation. The result became known as Scallop-gate. Without realising that the scallops he cooked alongside black pudding and hollandaise sauce had gone off, Tim proudly served his creation to Gordon. 'Fucking minging,' was all Gordon could say, before rushing outside to try to throw them back up in full view of the cameras.

'It wasn't exactly the best start it could have been. I felt a bit sick myself,' Tim admitted afterwards. 'I thought, Oh my God, I've poisoned Gordon Ramsay, and I felt terrible.'

But the young chef would soon be feeling a whole lot worse. Next under the Ramsay microscope came the kitchen itself. And it turned out that the rancid scallops weren't the only horrors on the shelves. Mouldy strawberries, rotting tomatoes, ingrained dirt, grime and grease. Having bitten his tongue to keep the nervous television producers happy, Gordon finally let rip.

'I've got a good fucking mind to get hold of fucking Sue and just tell her to fucking shut the place. This is the fucking pits. I've never seen anything like this in my entire fucking life. This is a fucking disgrace and a fucking embarrassment to catering.'

With these seven f-words in less than a minute, British television passed a new milestone.

Tim, however, had more humiliations and X-rated ear-bashings in store. Giving him the benefit of the doubt, Gordon wanted to see if he could cook better at home than he could in the restaurant. But he couldn't. With Tim's parents and grandparents sitting alongside him, Gordon watched as the youngster let his croutons catch fire and saw his weekend roast end in disaster. The head chef who had started out washing dishes in a restaurant five years earlier appeared to have learned little of value since.

Back at the restaurant, Gordon put Tim alongside his fellow chef and best mate Lee Symonds to see how well the pair really knew their food. The blindfolded taste test proved his worst fears. Having told the chefs that they had to decide which of the dishes put in front of them was a rare and which a medium steak, Gordon replaced the beef with a plate of pork and a plate of lamb. Neither Tim nor Lee could taste the difference.

The locals in Silsden knew what they liked to eat, though – and it wasn't the fancy cuisine Tim aspired to. After working out what nearby restaurants served and what they charged for it, Gordon said he thought

Bonaparte's should focus on simpler, traditional Yorkshire fare. Tim didn't agree and another brilliant television moment was born. The pair headed out into the streets with a silver platter of food to see if the locals preferred Tim's complex cooking or Gordon's heartier beef and ale pie. 'One-nil, you Fucker!' Gordon crowed when the first customer picked the pie. 'Two fucking nil! Three-nil, you tosser!'

Then, with a final laugh, Gordon threw Tim's rejected food into the river.

Amazingly enough, as the humiliations went on, Gordon admitted that, despite all evidence to the contrary, he was actually holding himself in check. When he pushed Tim's head in a basin of whisked egg whites as a punishment for yet another perceived misdemeanour, he admitted, 'I only did it because I couldn't exactly ram a rolling pin up his arse on television.' And he says, when he got frustrated at the flamboyant way the youngster tossed a salad, he only just stopped himself from pushing the greens in the same direction.

More seriously, what really bothered Gordon was a growing fear that Tim didn't share his passion for food. For, without that, he felt he could never get through to him. 'Before I arrived at the restaurant on that first day, I had been told that all I had to do was strip away Tim's pretensions, that he had the makings of a great chef because he truly loved food. Did he fuck! He was in love with the notion of being famous, not with food. That seriously pissed me off. That sort of thing always has.'

The show, however, had to go on. And with it came the twist that made *Ramsay's Kitchen Nightmares* such compulsive television. The man who had shouted and sworn his kitchen companions into submission suddenly turned into their best friend and most loyal supporter. Nobody was beyond saving, he said. And he was ready to do whatever it took to do just that.

At Bonaparte's, that meant cleaning up the health-hazard kitchen and trying to give Tim some pride in his workplace. Next came a unique way to give the lacklustre chef some new drive and energy. 'You're fucking 21, for fuck's sake! You should be getting 12 fucking hard-ons a day,' Gordon yelled, dragging Tim out for a kickabout on a nearby football pitch. Swinging on the goalposts after scoring a goal, the former Rangers player tried desperately to fire up his young charge. And after a while he seemed to be succeeding.

A quieter and more intense Gordon gradually persuaded Tim to find fresher, simpler ingredients and to pick less demanding, more suitable recipes. He offered a mini-masterclass on how to taste and season food. It was real teaching and as a result real progress was made and real results achieved. On Valentine's Night, one of the most important dates in many restaurants' calendars, a rush of marketing meant the normally empty dining room at Bonaparte's was full. Diners seemed to like the new bistro look Gordon had picked, and the new, less fussy menu that reflected it. And in the kitchen a newly energised Tim and deputy Lee were firing on all cylinders, ready and able to serve 50 meals for the first time in their careers.

It was uplifting, exciting stuff, marked by tears, hugs and genuine pleasure on all sides. The simple conclusion was that Gordon had done his job. He had seen the problems, sorted them out and turned Bonaparte's around in less than two weeks. Show over. Or was it?

Immediately after Valentine's Day, a still outspoken Gordon headed back down south to leave the transformed Bonaparte's crew to it. 'They were lazy little fuckers and I had to go back to Claridge's and just watch the kitchen run like a beautiful machine, the dishes passing before my eyes, before I felt calm again,' he told friends afterwards.

But things were not as calm in Yorkshire. A month later, Gordon and the film crew were back to see if business was still booming. It wasn't.

Tim and Sue were back fighting each other about the way the kitchen and the restaurant should be run. The dirt, the grime and the piles of rotting food were back behind the scenes. And the customers had all but disappeared. Tim was on his way out and Bonaparte's, Sue said, was closing its doors for good.

At this stage, Tim was taking it all on the chin – though a war of words between him and Gordon would soon be played out in the tabloids as the youngster tried everything from getting on *GMTV* to getting into *Big Brother*. 'I can't cook as well as I thought I could, clearly, but I can cook a bit otherwise I would never earn a wage,' was his initial assessment of the lessons he had learned. 'I have damaged my reputation but it is not true I was sacked from the restaurant. I had already resigned.'

Interestingly enough, he and Gordon did share one surprising concern in the days after their show was broadcast. Tim was worried about what his mother would say now she had seen her son smoking on television, while Gordon was terrified about what his would say about his swearing.

'Wherever he learned to talk like that, it certainly wasn't at home,' was her initial verdict when reporters asked her for her views. 'I always make sure he says sorry if he uses any bad language in front of me.'

What the show's production company, Optomen, realised the moment the cameras had stopped rolling in Silsden was that in Gordon Ramsay they had a real, gold-plated star on their hands. So the show's original title, *Cutting the Mustard*, was thrown out and *Ramsay's Kitchen Nightmares* was born. The swearing, they decided, would just have to be seen as part of the package and they would take any official criticism as it came.

On an unofficial level, Gordon faced an immediate backlash from residents of Silsden and other viewers after the first show was aired. 'All Gordon Ramsay and the programme makers were after were ratings,' said Chris Bone, one of Tim's best mates, who had watched the Bonaparte's programme with horror. Other locals said Gordon had deliberately patronised the town's residents by suggesting they were too stupid to appreciate anything other than hotpot or fish and chips when they went out to dinner.

Some criticism was even more personal, however. 'Ramsay is just another fat millionaire going on television to make more money, humiliate people less fortunate than himself and try and keep everyone else in their place,' Terry Clarke from Ipswich wrote on the internet chatroom DigitalSpy. 'Just like Simon Cowell he doesn't care about anyone but himself, he doesn't know the first thing about hard work and he wouldn't last ten minutes in the real world.'

But Terry could hardly have been more wrong. Hard work had long since been imprinted in Gordon's DNA. He knew, and none better, how tough it is to come from nowhere and climb to the top of a profession where you have no friends, no contacts and no connections to help you. The failed footballer from a broken home on one of Glasgow's toughest estates had been fighting against the odds from the start. Whatever the critics might say, Gordon was the perfect person to show others how to overcome obstacles and turn their careers around. He had been doing that all his life.

When you take the time to find out where Gordon is from, what he has seen and how far he has travelled, it is little wonder that he's so angry. Little wonder he has no time for failure, for underperformance or for fools. And little wonder that he says bad language is one of the world's least important sins. As far as Gordon is concerned, 'hell's kitchen' wasn't just the title of some future television show. It was also the place that had first saved and then almost destroyed him. 'My life has been an incredible roller-coaster ride,' he said in 2005. That ride had taken in incredible highs and terrible lows. And it had begun almost 40 years earlier in a family that risked being torn apart by alcohol, violence, drugs and fear.

TWO

PLAYING FOR RANGERS

Egg and chips. Ham, egg and chips when Mum was feeling flush. Steak and chips with a fried egg on top on special occasions when Dad took the family out for cheap Sunday lunches at a local hotel. They are not the sort of mealtime memories you might expect to hear from the man who would turn out to be the highest-profile and most imaginative chef of his generation. But that was pretty much all Gordon Ramsay ate as a child in one of the toughest parts of Glasgow. That and tripe.

'We didn't have a lot of money, so it was a very hard upbringing with very limited food on the table,' he says. 'We never sat down to a starter, main course and pudding and we had to eat everything we were given. There was no such thing as "don't like" in our family. Tripe is the obvious example. It wasn't exactly anyone's favourite, but we had to eat it when we were served it. Mealtimes weren't exactly much fun back then.'

Gordon was born on 8 November 1966 and named after his hard-drinking, heavy-smoking father – a man who had swum for Scotland at the age of 15 and had seen life as a brutal competition ever since.

A PE teacher in a local school, Gordon Ramsay senior was as traditional and as chauvinistic as they come. His attitudes and rules were the only ones that mattered in the Ramsay household and from the start he made it clear that his elder son was never expected to do as much as boil an egg, let alone cook a proper meal. On the family's council estate, the idea was that men were men, and women, only women, were expected to spend their lives in a kitchen.

What the men could do, however, was go out to find food – as long as they killed it first. So Gordon, his younger brother Ronald and their dad would sometimes leave the rough city streets behind for a weekend's fly-fishing on the River Tay. They were rare peaceful days in a childhood where storms were brewing from the very start. Gordon says, even as a young boy, it was obvious to him that his father had an eye for other women, a problem with drink and a temper he could barely control. He was frustrated and angry at work and he brought all those feelings and more home with him – though it was to be many years before Gordon found out just how much his mother had suffered at his father's hands on those long Glasgow nights.

Like most men of his generation, Gordon's dad had two passions in life: music and football. Bored by the first, his son tried desperately to win his affection by sharing the second. The family were lifelong Rangers supporters and, after two seasons of begging to go to a match, Gordon finally got taken through the gates of Ibrox Park just after his seventh birthday. It was one of Scotland's big derbies, a sell-out clash between Glasgow Rangers and Hearts, and to this day Gordon remembers it as an ugly, dirty match played in front of a frightening, threatening and sporadically violent crowd. 'And I loved everything about it,' he says.

But thriving on that sort of experience at just seven years old wasn't enough to impress Gordon senior – because he hadn't been there to witness his young son's confidence. Instead, Gordon had watched the match from his Uncle Roland's shoulders and it was with his uncle that he would return to Ibrox again and again over the next two years. His dad, meanwhile, stayed at home brooding about the imagined slights he faced at work and the ways he could exact revenge.

Looking back, Gordon says he thinks staying in Scotland would have destroyed his father – and possibly everyone else in the family. But the Ramsays were to get a fresh start and a stay of execution. One day, Gordon's dad quit the job that was making him so miserable and took the family 300 miles south to Warwickshire, where he was to become manager of Stratford-upon-Avon's brand-new sports centre.

As far as young Gordon was concerned, their new home was another world – and hopefully a far safer one. 'Stratford is the most English of places and it was a huge culture shock after Glasgow,' he says. 'There were none of those enormous Glasgow buildings and no tubes and trains running everywhere. Glasgow was fierce – up there we shopped at the Barras outdoor market, but Stratford had supermarkets. It felt sophisticated, posh and a whole lot calmer.'

For a while, things were calmer at home as well. Gordon senior threw his energies into his new job and the whole family began to put down roots. Gordon grabbed the top bunk in the room he would share with Ronnie for much of the next decade and formed a gang of four with their elder sister Diane and younger sister Yvonne. With free access to their dad's leisure centre, it is little wonder that the kids were soon obsessed by sports – Gordon more than any of them.

What he wasn't as interested in was school. 'I got bored easily because I'm a real hot pants and I can't sit still for long. But I was fanatical about sport. In the afternoons, if I wasn't playing football, I was fishing off the weir or climbing up the side of the theatre and doing moonies and jumping in the Avon. We hunted for conkers outside Anne Hathaway's cottage and we all just had great fun.'

But, after a while, Gordon's dad lost his early enthusiasm for work and started to go back into his shell. So nine-year-old Gordon tried once more to please him and pull him back out of it. The youngster had seen that going to football matches hadn't worked. So he thought that some direct competition might do the trick instead. 'Almost every day I would run up alongside the edge of the 25-metre pool to see if I could run faster than Dad could swim,' he says. He never could – and Gordon senior never once thought to boost his son's confidence by slowing down.

What also drove Gordon forward was a sense that he was always one step behind his younger brother in the quest for his father's affection. 'Ronnie was always Dad's blue-eyed boy. He was Number One. Definitely the favourite.' So Gordon decided to run faster, climb higher, do whatever it took to overtake his brother. 'My big thing was cross-country racing on the edge of town at Coughton, which was one of Warwickshire's toughest races. The course was nine miles and covered all terrains: forests, fields, streams, country lanes, corn, sheep, farmyards and suddenly back into the school grounds. It was tough but I was desperate to win it.'

But, even if he had come first, Gordon reckons his dad would hardly have noticed. There had to be something else, he thought, some other talent he had buried inside him which would make his father sit up and pay attention. Kicking a football around their housing estate one day, Gordon reckoned he might have found it. Every boy in the country kicks a football about as a child. Probably every boy hopes he's better than all the other kids on the estate. But Gordon suddenly realised that in his case it was true. He really could kick the ball harder, faster and more accurately than anyone else. He could keep possession of it even when the older kids tried to steal it from him. He could pass the ball wherever and whenever he wanted. He could run like hell with it. He could score goals. If I train harder, he thought, this has got to be something Dad will approve of.

But Gordon senior didn't seem to notice his son's new obsession – or his talent. Because he had a new obsession of his own: he wanted to be in a band and he didn't care what effect this dream would have on his family. 'You'd come home on a Saturday afternoon, having played football, and Dickie Davies would be on telly, and while you tried to watch the results Dad would suddenly be trying to show you he was a better guitarist than Hank Marvin,' says Gordon, able to laugh at the early days of his dad's transformation. 'Then every Sunday Dad had the music blaring out. It was that council-house thing of the windows open, the fucking speakers were on and who has got the loudest stereo.'

But bigger problems started to build up when Gordon senior joined a local band. 'We'd have to go to these social clubs where he was playing gigs. We'd be bored stiff, then we'd have to help lift all these amps and speakers down the stairs and into the van. And I knew what would have happened along the way. Mum would have got agitated because someone would have eyed Dad up, and then when he had a drink he was like a different person and everything changed. The hell he put my mum through back then…' Gordon's voice tailed off, still unable to share some of the worst memories of his childhood.

What seemed clear to everyone in the family except Gordon senior was the fact that his dreams of music stardom were always going to be dashed. Before he was even a teenager, Gordon reckoned he could smell failure – and he hated it. 'Dad was never going to be a professional musician. The best he managed was working men's clubs – playing alongside Marty Wilde on a couple of occasions. I would sit in all those smoky rooms listening to him playing on a stool with a synthesiser, strutting his stuff, and I knew it was never going to be.' Gordon senior, however, would go on trying to keep his dream alive – whatever the consequences for his wife and kids.

'At one point he sold the family car to pay for a ticket to Texas, where he had planned to spend three months playing with a band. The first everyone else in the family knew what he had done was when the finance company turned up to collect the keys.' The event had been a big wake-up call for the family. 'You just don't forget those kinds of situations,' said Gordon later. 'Mum struggling to pay the bills and putting up with all this shit. It was embarrassing when the school had a holiday trip as well. There was no point in my bringing a form home to ask if I could go because then the rest of the kids would have to go and there was no way we could afford it. You learn, even at 12 and 13, that this is not the way to go in life. My father taught me a lot, without telling me anything at all.'

Over the years, the Ramsay family have rarely talked about their other, far lower points. 'There was violence and sadness and happiness combined in one house,' was all Gordon would offer when asked about it years later. But, when trying to raise money for women's refuge centres and for helplines for child victims of domestic violence, Gordon has also described the pain of seeing his mother wearing a pair of sunglasses in the middle of November after saying she had tripped on the stairs or walked into a door. And the times she dragged the whole family out of the house at 2.30 in the morning to get to a secure housing unit to escape any further beatings.

But what Helen Ramsay also did, for so many years, was to go back to her husband time and time again. Today Gordon says he can only applaud what may seem a dangerous and self-destructive decision. 'The reason she seemed so weak was because she was defending our arses.

You have to admire the loyalty of a woman who puts her children first. And that's where I get my determination from. From her, without a doubt.'

This determination was what made the teenage Gordon work even harder out on the football pitch. He still believed it wasn't too late to break through to his father and, like many children from a violent home, he believed that if his dad was proud of his son his mother might get left alone. So Gordon aimed high. He wouldn't just stop at the school and county teams he had been targeting so far. Instead, he would fight his way into the family team back in Scotland. He made a vow to get signed for Glasgow Rangers. Surely nothing could make his dad prouder than that.

At 14, Gordon took a huge step in that direction, starting to travel up to Glasgow every school holiday to train with the club in the hope of being taken on as part of the full Youth Training Scheme. He was entitled to wear an official club blazer on each visit and found out how it feels to run out into a stadium that can seat more than 51,000. But he didn't get called back when the last of the holiday sessions were over and he braced himself for the disappointment, contempt or worse he knew he would see in his dad's eyes at the news.

What he didn't do, though, was give up. He had fought his way into his school team years ahead of most of the other players and he carried the battle on until he represented his county as well. He then tried out and was signed for various local semi-professional teams as he prepared to leave school at 16. 'I was naturally aggressive, a left-back and a cut-throat tackler. You may have got past once but there was never, ever a second occasion. And I was fast, a great 100-metre sprinter. I did well.'

Well enough to catch Rangers' eye again. A scout watched him play in a local youth game and called him back up to Ibrox for one final shot at the big time. As he walked back into the club grounds that day, Gordon knew the next few hours would be the most important of his life. Already coming up to 16, he was at the upper age limit if he wanted to break into the professional game. This was make or break time and he was going to give it everything he had.

'Even if they didn't like my game, they must have still liked my attitude,' he told his uncle afterwards.

But the Rangers staff had given him no clues about how well he had done, so he headed back down to Stratford to wait. And to wait. In the end, just over four weeks passed before a letter with a Glasgow postmark landed on the Ramsay doormat. Gordon says that at first he was too nervous to open it and the rest of the family were too nervous to force him. But, when he did, the news was good.

'They had invited me to come to Glasgow on a year's apprenticeship, then, if it went well, as a reserve-team player,' he says.

He wasn't being given a contract or any real commitment. But he was on his way and he wasn't going to be left on his own. Despite everyone's objections, his parents decided that the whole family would have to leave their home, their friends, their jobs and their schools. Everyone would move back north to support Gordon. It turned out to be a decision that would ultimately destroy the family and leave Gordon repaying psychological debts for most of the next decade. And almost immediately the cracks began to show.

'I was acutely aware of the responsibility I was carrying for the whole family having been uprooted and for the first three months I absolutely hated my new life. My mother wasn't happy either and I could see that my father had a growing problem with alcohol now he was back in Scotland. He could no longer have just one or two glasses – he always had to finish the bottle. He would drink himself into a stupor and then the country and western music would go on. They were not good times for any of us.'

The irony of this only intensified the depression and insecurity Gordon was already feeling. Just as he had finally started to do something he thought his father would have to be proud of, the older man started to retreat from the world and blot it all out. Far from halting the violence Gordon's mother suffered at home, as her son had hoped, the move back to Glasgow seemed to have made matters worse. And things weren't a lot better at training. 'I got the shit kicked out of me at Rangers,' he admits. 'They didn't believe I was born in Glasgow because of my Stratford accent, and I didn't fit in with their lifestyle of playing pool, getting pissed and eating pies.'

Meanwhile, Gordon's elder sister, Diane, had persuaded her parents that she should be allowed to stay at college in Banbury, near Stratford, after all. The family was falling apart. And Gordon thought it was all his fault. The only way he could make amends, he believed, was to make it into the first team and become a success. Failure suddenly wasn't an option. He had to make it so he could buy houses for his parents, his brother and his sisters, the way you read that other footballers did. Gordon Ramsay, always in a hurry, was more ambitious and resolute than ever.

'I was a pretty determined player and I was becoming pretty nasty,' he says when asked to describe his game back then. 'They called me "Flash" because I was fast and if I were to compare myself with any more recent footballers I'd say I was most like Stuart Pearce.' Whose nickname, of course, was 'Psycho'.

But after a few reserve-team games Gordon realised he wasn't the only person in the squad with a temper. Whenever he is criticised for the way he treats his staff in the kitchen, he says what he does is nothing compared with the way managers and trainers treat their teams at half-time. And at Ibrox he met his first management role model: former player Jock Wallace. 'He was fucking ruthless, a Scottish version of Mike Tyson. When he wanted to rip your arse out, he would crucify you,' is how Gordon remembers the overall mood in the dressing room. And, while he admits the stress of fighting for selection made him physically ill, he was still thriving on the pressure and riding with the punches.

Now he really was on the brink of making it big. He got into the main 18-strong squad and by the end of his first season in Scotland he had played two first-team games, one against St Johnstone, the other against Morton – the club that years later he would be rumoured to be buying.

'The St Johnstone friendly was the first time I played with Ally McCoist. Davie Cooper, Ian Ferguson and Derek Ferguson were just through in the year above me, so even though I didn't play the full game it was all a dream for a kid like me.' But very soon it was all going to turn into a nightmare.

Just as Gordon was getting ready for his third first-team appearance and was cementing his position in the main Rangers squad, he smashed the cartilage in his knee and was out of the game for 11 long weeks. Then he made matters worse by ignoring the medical advice he had been given about letting the joint rest. 'There was no such thing as keyhole surgery in those days and I tried to come back too soon after the accident. Seven months after it had happened, very stupidly, I played a game of squash. I tore a cruciate ligament and was then in plaster for another four months.'

For a professional sportsman, this kind of long layoff is almost unbearable. 'So many things go through your mind, your confidence is wiped out and you become paranoid,' Gordon said of his own experience. He was convinced that his former colleagues were moving forward while he was falling back. He was terrified that a newcomer might steal his place on the bench. And, worst of all, he was afraid that he might never regain his old match-fitness.

Unfortunately for Gordon, it looked like he was right about his fitness. When the plaster was taken off his leg and his rehab was finished, he threw himself back into training, desperate to prove that he could recover and pick up where he had left off. But deep down he knew his leg no longer felt the same. He spent hours in hot and then cold baths after training sessions, trying everything he could think of to dull the new pains and pretend they didn't matter. Mentally, he was determined to be as tough as ever and he was staking everything on a career-making third main-team appearance at Ibrox.

But, at the start of the following season, he was told it was never going to happen. Jock Wallace and his assistant Archie Knox called the 19-year-old into their office at 10am on a Friday and broke the news. It was all over. Gordon was out of the main team and his contract wasn't being renewed. He remembers the words hitting him like a physical blow – and to this day he refuses to hold business meetings on Friday mornings in case the memories of that initial rejection come flooding back. At the time, he just gripped the edges of his chair and tried to hide his feelings. 'I sat and thought, You bastards, looking at them both, and while I wanted to cry I wouldn't give them the pleasure of doing it in front of them. The whole meeting probably didn't last more than five minutes but when it was over every dream I'd ever had had been taken away.'

And Gordon was convinced that the dream really was over. Wallace and Knox suggested he do more rehab, move down a league, join another club to get match-fit and then prove he was good enough to play for Rangers again at a later date. The door, they said, would always be open for him. But Gordon refused even to think about it. 'I said no, straight away. I'm an all-or-nothing guy and I knew that, if I couldn't play for Rangers, then forget it. I wasn't about to scrape £45 a week for the next ten years. I didn't want to play for some Sunday team somewhere else instead. I wanted to throw my boots away and to retire from football altogether.'

But first he wanted to get over the shock of being rejected. 'I went home, sat down and finally started to cry.

I wanted to attack the whole world. I really thought I could make it with Rangers because I knew I was one of their better young players. It was devastating and I had a serious breakdown. I was too upset to talk to anyone and bawled my eyes out in private for the whole weekend. I thought, Christ, that's it. All my mates know. What do I do now? The sense of rejection was humiliating, awful, and I took the failure very, very badly, like any 18-year-old would. I couldn't move on and I wanted to forget about it.'

What he needed more than anything was support from his dad. But he didn't get it. 'Dad had been sitting in his van just outside the grounds when I got the news from Wallace and telling him was the worst thing I had done. Again I wouldn't give him the pleasure of seeing me cry. He never said anything good, and from the moment we left Ibrox his attitude was clear. "You get yourself into another club," he said. "You continue hounding Rangers. You get your knee working, start kicking with your right foot and stop putting so much emphasis on being a naturally left-footed player." Even though he had hardly come to watch any of my matches, Dad wanted me to continue living the dream. He would have been happy to have me playing in a lower league – part-time footballer, part-time insurance man or something. But I'd learned the football was never really going to work. I was always going to be stuck with the label "gammy knee". So I had to let go of what I loved first, and that was hard. I'd been so close. And I felt so bitter for so long.'

The embarrassment of seeing his dad try and fail to make it in the music business was another reason why Gordon was determined to make a clean break from football. 'He had followed a dream everyone knew was never going to come true and I already knew that I didn't want to turn out like him. I dropped football like a fucking lead balloon because I knew it wasn't going to come true either.'

And, while Gordon tried to work out what the hell he could do instead, he saw his family and his personal life start to fall apart. His dad's drinking had hit new heights, while the way he treated his wife and family had hit new lows. He was having an affair at work and was refusing to contribute to the housekeeping budget even though the final reminders were piling up. Unable to shake off his own depression, Gordon split up with the girlfriend he had been dating for nearly four years.

'Although the football pressure was gone I felt the family pressure more. Dad was still doing nothing but criticise me – at one point, he even suggested that I was exaggerating the injuries. Now I look back and wonder how any father can be so unsupportive and unloving towards his injured son. I know it's an awful thing to say but I was beginning to despise him. A month later, our relationship had deteriorated so much that I knew I had to get out and I went to stay with my sister Diane down in Banbury.

'Shortly after that, I got a call from Yvonne to tell me that Mum was having to wear sunglasses again to disguise the bruises on her face. As if that wasn't enough, Dad had also stopped paying the mortgage, so the building society repossessed the house – the home of her own that my mother had longed for all her life. She was humiliated again, and her dream was shattered.'

Amazingly, the family stayed together. They all moved to

a five-bedroom council house in Bridgwater, in Somerset, and Gordon's mum found new work – ironically, in a women's refuge run by social services which Gordon still supports financially to this day.

Meanwhile, Gordon had stumbled upon an idea of what he might do next. Before moving up to Glasgow, his mother had worked at the Cobweb Tea Rooms, in Sheep Street in the middle of Stratford. With their oak beams, low ceilings and traditional menus, the tea rooms were the ultimate in hushed English gentility. But, when he had visited his mum there on Saturday afternoons, Gordon had found out that behind the scenes it was a completely different story. In the kitchen, there was activity, panic, energy. Everyone seemed to be moving at once, everyone had a role and everyone was simultaneously an individual and part of a team. It's a football team, Gordon had realised, in a moment of revelation. If I'm not going to be a professional sportsman, I'd be happy to work here, he thought at the time – which was one reason why he'd enrolled at a catering college in Oxford just before being called up to Ibrox at 16.

Nearly four years later, he wondered if he would get the same buzz out of that kind of environment. After he left Rangers, the Police and the Royal Navy had both turned him down on finding out he had failed all but two of his O levels, and now he was struggling for both money and direction. Desperate for cash, he got a part-time job in a restaurant and fell in love again with the environment. It would change his life. 'That year, I had six weeks of being a waiter, which was a disaster. I only lasted four days working the tables and spent the rest of the time in the kitchen. And I loved it. I loved it instantly, big time. The boisterousness, the hassle, the shouting, the screaming, the activity. I found a sense of freedom there.'

Some of the kitchen staff suggested he reconsider full-time catering training and found him details of a foundation course he could try. And the more Gordon learned about it, the more he thought they might be right. But this time he knew he had to be sure before signing up. 'Now the football had ended I knew that I couldn't afford to mess up a second time. That very first day after I had been kicked out of Rangers I can remember sitting down and thinking to myself, OK, the next thing I do, I've got to get it right. I was obsessed with never again being told that I'm not good enough. I had failed once in life. I swore I would never fail at anything ever again.'

If the 19-year-old Gordon Ramsay was indeed going to become a chef, he wanted to be the best chef in the world. 'If I can't have an FA Cup winner's medal, I want a third Michelin star,' he said years later when he realised how he could prove himself and be measured against the best in his new industry. Back in Bridgwater, Gordon had a few more hurdles to cross before he got on to the HND course in catering management he was interested in. All of them were about the way other people would treat his decision. The main one, not surprisingly, involved his father – the man who years ago had put extra salt on his son's porridge 'so as not to produce a wuss'.

Even after so many disappointments, so many examples of how not to behave, Gordon still felt he needed his father's blessing. He never got it. 'Dad was a very stubborn man and for him it was always football or nothing. He'd had a tough time with his own father, a butcher. And when I tested the water by saying, "Dad, I get excited by being in a boisterous kitchen, I want to be a chef," he flipped his lid. He was a very macho man, the toughest, and he thought catering was for poofs. It was one thing to tell his mates that his son was playing for Rangers, but quite another to say I was training to be a cook. "Stay away from catering," he said to me at one point. "It's girly and effeminate." I don't think he ever really forgave me when I ignored him.'

Unfortunately, the same message was coming from many of Gordon's friends as well. And it was coming through especially loud and clear from his former teammates at Rangers. 'I knew it would be hard to go from wearing that amazing strip to putting a pinny on,' he said. 'But I never thought it was girly, even though Ally McCoist and a whole load of the big-name players said I was a poof.'

With the decision made, Gordon enrolled on his course, swore he would make the best of it and got an immediate boost. 'The day our lecturer started screaming at us all because we weren't showing enough interest, I was hooked. I also got excited when I found out the amount of freedom involved around food – each and every season is different, each and every customer is different. It became my obsession. My escape from watching Mum and Dad waste their lives and witnessing him trying to destroy her mentally. I had no idea I was going to be good at it but I loved it from day one.'

Customers, however, may have had different ideas about his suitability for the job – and Gordon is happy to admit that his first ventures weren't entirely successful. 'I remember one day I made apple pie to be served with Sunday lunch. The pastry had shrunk – a bit of a disaster. I made mint sauce but by mistake used washing-up liquid instead of vinegar – a total disaster.'

Even so, after a year's study, he gained his HND in catering management while working part-time in a small country house hotel just outside Stratford. He was on his way – and people who knew him realised he was going to move fast. William Murray, immediately nicknamed Minty by Gordon, was at Banbury Technical College with him and also cooked with him at the army barracks at Folkestone in the summer of 1984. He says Gordon had long since got to grips with what you had to achieve to succeed in the restaurant world. Second best was never going to be enough for him, so working away in a distinctly average restaurant was never going to be on the menu. 'Even then Gordon made it clear he wanted nothing less than his own place with three Michelin stars. He was quite prepared to put in the 16-plus-hour days and take the abuse young chefs get in order to fulfil his ambitions.'

But William admits there were never any guarantees that it would work out for Gordon. 'He was a bit of a nutter even then and I knew he was either going to end up in prison or make a million. I'm just pleased it was the latter,' he told the BBC years later.

Other people were also pleased to see their faith in Gordon repaid that summer. The local branch of the Round Table had stepped in to help when Gordon realised he couldn't afford the chef's clothes, knives and other kit he needed for his year at college. 'They paid for the whole thing and if it hadn't been for them I wouldn't be where I am today.'

Before heading out into the world of full-time work, Gordon made one final bid to make peace with his father. Looking back, he says he knows it was crazy to keep on trying – and that he should have guessed that once more he would have the door shut in his face. 'As ever, it all meant nothing to my father,' he said after graduating from college, for which he had hoped for some paternal praise. 'He still could not understand for a moment how any real man could be interested in food. I felt sad that, yet again, he had failed to support me. For, in spite of everything he had said or done to hurt me and his family, my father still remained the bedrock of my world and his approval still mattered to me.'

Or at least it did until the phone rang late one night. 'Ronnie called to say that Mum had been hospitalised for two days as a result of another attack by my father. I remember calling Dad then and there and telling him that he was no longer my father. At that point, I honestly never wanted to see him again and we were all relieved when we found out he had run away to Spain with another woman.'

Meanwhile, Ronnie was starting to have problems of his own. At 16, before working as a mechanic and briefly being in the Army, he had started smoking marijuana. Nobody really gave it a second thought at the time. Nobody realised that for Ronnie this first soft drug really would lead to other, far more serious addictions. As for Gordon, the summer of 1986 was to prove another major turning point in his life. He had read voraciously of some of the great chefs working in London, Paris, New York and other capitals around the world. For all the amazing work they did, many of them were known only to their peers in the restaurant business and to real restaurant fans. Some had been on television, become famous and made a nice amount of money. But, as far as Gordon could tell, there was no real Premier League of chefs to generate a proper sense of competition in the industry. From his bedroom in Banbury, the former footballer decided to create one.

THREE

HARD SLOG AND BAD LANGUAGE

When you are brought up on a council estate and learn your trade out in the sticks, you tend to have high expectations of what you will find if you ever make it to the bright lights of the capital. So the teenage Gordon Ramsay was hoping to see great things when he got his first job in a London kitchen. Instead, he got a very nasty shock.

In the mid-1980s, good British restaurants remained few and far between. Cooking, Gordon discovered, still pretty much meant pouring sauces on to reheated legs of lamb or pieces of beef that had been roasted and sliced the previous day. Vegetables might be overcooked, but by the time they got to a diner's plate they were lukewarm. Decent presentation was ignored, service was appalling and nobody seemed to think anything was wrong.

For several months, Gordon wondered if he had made a

huge mistake by picking this as his new career. Had he been imagining things when he had seen all that excitement in the kitchens of his childhood? Did no one in London share his passion for food and for how it could be created, presented and enjoyed? As Gordon would ultimately find out, a small number of top chefs did. But they too say they had to fight against the grim, traditional attitudes and practices that were already giving Gordon sleepless nights.

'All the top London hotels served the same food when I first came to London,' says Anton Mosimann, one of the early super-chefs credited with transforming the capital's moribund restaurant scene. 'The Savoy, the Ritz, Claridge's – there was no difference. The chefs had all worked there for many years and their attitude was: this is the system, why change it?

'I found that the lamb, for instance – and it was always a saddle of lamb – was cooked each morning at 5am, taken out of the oven at 7am, carved, covered in foil, kept warm and then served at 8pm. Very unhappy-looking meat. And that was it. The rice was also cooked a day in advance. There was no fresh food cooked to order. When diners asked what vegetables were being served, the waiters would reply, "Today we have peas, carrots, peas, beans, peas." They were determined to serve peas. And the peas were frozen.'

Anton fought against the prevailing wisdom by tearing up the rulebook and forcing through his vision of lower-fat, freshly cooked food. And Gordon was determined to follow in the older man's footsteps. Having been turned down by the Royal Navy two years earlier, he organised the next steps of his career with the precision of a military campaign.

While working at the Intercontinental Hotel and in his other job at Maxim's de Paris in London, Gordon spent hours working out which were the capital's best and most innovative restaurants. He already knew what he would need to learn if he were ever to run one of them. And he wanted to make sure he knew exactly whom he could learn it from. 'I believe that, if you want to be the best, then you have to work for the best. If you do, there's no automatic assumption that you will make it. But that's where you have to start.'

At the top of Gordon's list as a possible mentor was Leeds-born Marco Pierre White, the man who had made headlines and won awards with the launch of Harvey's in south London's then unfashionable Wandsworth. At 25, Marco was only five years older than Gordon, but he was already seen as one of the country's new generation of super-chefs. And, as soon as Gordon clapped eyes on him, he knew he had found a soul mate. A hero had been born.

'Marco had long hair. He looked like he'd done ten rounds with Mike Tyson. I thought, Christ, I want to work for that guy.' Cooking, for a man like that, really could be rock and roll, Gordon decided. It would be worlds away from the pre-heated meats and overcooked sauces that were already starting to drive him mad. But how could he make the move?

In the end, Gordon just rang the normal booking number for Harvey's, demanded to speak to Marco, spun some lies about his experience and qualifications and was given a few trial shifts where he could try to prove his worth. Looking back, he says he knew he was in the right place from the very first morning in south London – not least because the atmosphere in the kitchen was as tense and exciting as he had hoped for. He says everyone there seemed to have a temper, everyone swore constantly, everyone shouted and screamed at one another. And, while Gordon was at the bottom of the pile and the focus of much of the aggression, he knew immediately that he would thrive on it.

'The most important thing for a chef is that you've got to be able to take a bollocking. The trick is to remember that none of the insults is meant to be personal. Bollocking worked with me. I've been slapped and kicked and punched. And when the chef shouted at me, I listened, took it in and said, "Oui, chef." When I was training, a bollocking made me try harder. At Harvey's, I took the flak till the cows came home. Marco pushed me as far as possible; it was a test of strength and yes we went to the limit and yes I know it was worth it.'

Gordon stayed at Harvey's for nearly two long years, working 17-hour days, learning his craft, storing up information and experiences and helping make some of the capital's freshest, most exciting meals. It was tough, exhausting and the money was lousy. But Gordon loved every minute. 'For the first time in years I felt secure,' he said. 'Good at what I was doing and happy in myself.' But he still kept his private life and his professional life separate. The kitchen gang used to get together for football games in the afternoons and at weekends – but Gordon was determined to make sure his boss never found out about his past at Rangers. 'I was terrified that one day Marco might turn around and say, "You were a failed footballer, and now you are a failed chef", so I kept that part of my life secret.'

Working for a man like Marco Pierre White was never going to be enough for Gordon, though. He wanted to *be* a man like Marco Pierre White. So both of them knew that after a couple of years he would have to move on. To his credit, Marco had seen the potential in his younger apprentice. He saw how hard the man was prepared to work and how much abuse he was prepared to accept to produce the best possible food. So he decided to help him. As a first step, he put him in touch with the even more legendary Roux brothers.

The Frenchmen, Michel and Albert, had reportedly said that in moving to Britain their life's mission had been to convert 'a nation of culinary barbarians into one of gourmets'. By the time Gordon met them they were well on their way. Le Gavroche, their flagship restaurant in Mayfair, had won almost every award going and the brothers were famous for encouraging younger chefs to fulfil their potential through their Continental-style apprenticeship schemes.

'There was no better or more exciting place in the business to be,' Gordon said of his nearly 18 months at Le Gavroche. But both he and the Roux brothers knew he had far more still to learn. Michel and Albert were well known for having an amazing eye for spotting talent – and for working out how their proteges could smooth out any rough edges and fulfil their potential. They said Gordon needed to spread his wings and gain international experience among some other grand masters. They said he

which looks pretty when it gets to your table. There has to be much, much more to a top chef than style. The content has to be spot on as well.'

Behind the scenes, things were as manic and angry as they had been in London, though for Gordon there was one key difference. 'I couldn't speak a word of French when I arrived there. But it meant, thankfully, that I couldn't understand a word when I was being yelled at, which was nice.' As well as learning French – which Gordon lapses into all the time when shouting at his restaurant staff to this day – he also learned a little more about the work ethic required to become a top chef. It is a story he would ultimately tell in his cookbook *Kitchen Heaven*.

'When I was training with Guy Savoy I arrived one Friday morning feeling exhausted at the end of a busy week. I made the mistake of telling him so. "What do you mean, tired?" he said. "How many hours did you sleep?" I told him just six. "Six? That's far too many. By the time you get to 60 you'll have slept for 15 years. Does that scare you?"

'"Yes," I replied.

'"Well, then, shut the fuck up, sleep for four hours and by the time you reach 60 you'll only have slept for ten."'

As a still sleepy commis chef, the first rung of the career ladder for newly trained workers, Gordon was paid one of the lowest wages allowed by the French government – even though he was working in arguably the greatest French restaurant in the world. Like Ewan McGregor and Nicole Kidman's characters in the film *Moulin Rouge*, Gordon and his girlfriend lived in a bedsit on the top floor of a classic tenement block near the Paris Opera.

'Romantic and, better still, cheap' was how he described it at the time.

On his one weekly day off Gordon got a second job in the neighbourhood. He served coffee and emptied ashtrays at La Bastille, the grand old cafe opposite the Opera. But, while the tips could sometimes be generous, survival was still pretty hard. Every now and then, Gordon recalls, he would empty his pockets and wonder about what might have been. He reckons he was making a maximum of around £100 a week when some of his former teammates at Rangers were not only collecting £5,000 but also enjoying the adulation of thousands of fans. 'It was hard and it hurt to think of it,' he says. 'But I became even more determined not to fail again.'

His determination to learn and to carry on paying his dues was also as strong as ever. So he left Guy Savoy to work for another celebrated Frenchman: the Michelin star-holding Joel Robuchon, who had recently been named 'Chef of the Century' in Paris. And Gordon admits he had a very bad start. On his first day in Robuchon's kitchen, the chef threw a plate of langoustine ravioli at Gordon's head – because his foie gras sauce had spilled and the presentation was not up to scratch. 'I was 24 then – what could I do?' Gordon later said of the incident. 'Should I have thought that I was too good to take that? I wanted to learn from this guy, he was the best chef in the world and that was the price you pay. My ears got burned by the cabbage and I had all the stuff in my hair but I just said, "I'll make you another one right away, chef." I certainly didn't start crying on the phone to my mum. I just got on with it.'

Back in Britain, the powers that be had started to notice Gordon – and they approved of his desire to learn from the masters in France. He won a minor award as a top young apprentice and headed back to London to collect the prize and, more importantly, the prize money. It wasn't much, but it was enough to supplement his subsistence wages in France and it allowed him to stay there for another year. It was, he says, time well spent. 'The two and half years I had in France were the most important cooking years of my life,' he said later. 'The French have cooking at the forefront of their psyche and I was encouraged to feel the same. I built some fantastic foundations for my future in those years.'

And still the learning went on. Desperate for money rather than big kitchen experience, Gordon took Marco Pierre White's advice again and agreed to a well-paid private commission. He headed out to live on a yacht as personal chef to Reg Grundy, the Australian television magnate famous for giving the world *Neighbours* and Kylie Minogue. They sailed around the Mediterranean from the chic ports of Sardinia and Sicily to Corsica and Cannes and even crossed the Atlantic to the glorious British Virgin Islands and Antigua. As a crewmember, you can be fantastically busy when the boss, his family, friends or colleagues are on board. But at other times you can live like a king, get a great tan and experience the good life.

The job gave Gordon the diving bug, a sport he still loves today. It also helped him repay some of his debts, showed him how the other half lived and made him even more determined to become his own boss and make his own money. As soon as possible.

What he knew he wanted more than anything at this point was a restaurant of his own. A place in London where he could take on the masters and prove he had learned all their lessons. A place where he could make a real name for himself.

But, when you are a boy from a council estate in Glasgow who has had to wait at table just to afford your rent, it is hard to see how this kind of dream can become a reality. Setting up a London restaurant could cost hundreds of thousands of pounds even then. Gordon knew he had to try to call in some favours. He would beg and borrow the money. If it came to it, maybe he would even steal.

Interestingly, bearing in mind how volatile their relationship was to become in the years ahead, it was Marco Pierre White who came up trumps and helped Gordon into his first restaurant. A site had become available at 11 Park Walk, in Fulham. It was set on a side street off the noisy, traffic-filled Fulham Road. And it had bad vibes and a tricky history. Many a restaurant had opened there and soon closed after failing to attract enough paying customers. Big hopes in that corner of west London had often led to big losses – which is one reason why the plot was vacant yet again back in early 1993.

Everyone in the industry knew it would take something special to go against the trend and defy history. Could 26-year-old Gordon provide the X factor? Marco had lined up some other financial backers to help raise the funds for the venture, and Gordon himself borrowed as heavily as the banks would allow him. Everything he had, and a lot that he didn't, would be going on the line over the next 12 months.

Picking a name for a new restaurant is never easy. But Gordon and the team got that job done quickly. They wanted a single word that suggested health, freshness and something very slightly different. They reckoned they had it when someone suggested the name of a vegetable that was also a colour. Gordon's favourite colour, as it turned out – Aubergine.

Even Gordon himself says now that he's not sure exactly what it was that made the place such a big hit. In fitting out the room, he and his partners had tried to make it as airy as possible and give it a Mediterranean feel. When it came to the food Gordon's keyword was simplicity – and, years ahead of the rest of the world, his twin aims were to use as little fat in the dishes as possible and to keep the flavours as light and natural as he could. 'People come here for a three-course meal but I don't want them to feel heavy or overly full at the end,' he said. What he did want, though, was to come up with a personal signature. 'Over the years I have begged for as many menus from other places as possible to try and work out what they were all about. Now I want my cooking to be able to say: "That's me on the plate."'

One way he set himself apart was by taking simple, surprisingly cheap ingredients and somehow turning them into something special. 'How many London restaurants have mackerel on the menu?' he asked once when trying to make the point. His choices – of eight dishes for the main course, five of them fish – changed every three months, though what had turned into his signature dish, 'roast seabass with braised salsify and jus vanilla', tended to keep its place, as loyal customers asked for it even when it wasn't available.

The one thing that was always there was Gordon himself. 'People spend big money for a meal for two to know that I'm cooking the food,' he said. 'My chefs don't want to see me upstairs drinking Champagne. People don't wait for two months to eat cock-up food that hasn't been checked by me personally. It has to be perfect.'

To make sure it was, he tended to arrive at the restaurant at 8.30 in the morning to look at the day's menus, check the fresh food that was coming in, go over the books and the paperwork from the night before and deal with any management issues that needed tackling. Then came the food itself, as he got going on the lunch and then the dinner service. Most nights he would still be at 11 Park Walk nearly 18 hours after he had first arrived – and less than seven before he would be back in the kitchen to do it all again. It was relentless, exhausting, but exhilarating. At just 26, Gordon was head chef in his own London restaurant. He was living his dream. And the world was starting to notice both what he cooked and what he looked like.

Earning recognition for his food was the most important thing for him. And Fay Maschler, the celebrated restaurant critic of the *Evening Standard*, was one of the first to give him the seal of approval – something she might have regretted years later when Gordon turned on her in one of his periodic attacks on the critics. 'Certain dishes are straight copies of the masters but come excitingly reasonably priced. It's couture cooking at off-the-peg prices,' she wrote back in 1994 in a long, positive review. Perhaps equally important to Gordon's vanity was the sudden interest in his appearance. And he decided he might as well milk it as much as possible to get extra publicity for his restaurant.

'Gordon Ramsay is 6ft 2in, beefy, with natural fair hair and electric blue eyes. He talks about deep-sea diving, squash and working out. He doesn't smoke nor, interestingly, does he drink. Unless you have seen him in his chef's apron you would never guess that he cooks, or that he is about to become London's most chic chef,' wrote Pauline Peters, also in the *Evening Standard*. 'He is about as opposite to his mentor, the pallid and volatile Marco Pierre White, as it is possible to be.'

Meanwhile, the *Daily Telegraph* said Gordon looked more like 'a sportsman in fancy dress' with 'muscles straining against his chef's whites', rather than the traditional image of a well-fed restaurateur.

It hardly matters now whether it was Fay Maschler's review of his food or Pauline Peters's description of his looks that did the trick. The phones at Aubergine had started to ring – and for a long time they hardly stopped. After his six-year apprenticeship, Gordon had become an overnight sensation and his momentum seemed unstoppable. For ten straight months, he says, there was hardly ever an empty table at dinner – and one night he had 75 people on his waiting list for a restaurant that had already filled every one of its 45 seats. Long before eBay had been invented, some clever people were trying to cash in on Aubergine's sudden success by making Saturday-night bookings and placing adverts in London papers saying the reservations were now on sale to the highest bidders. Even his mother, who wanted to turn up and surprise him on his birthday during one of her rare forays into London, had to hang on the phone and wait for a cancellation.

Throughout all this, Gordon was thriving. But he admits his personal life was suffering. He split up with his latest girlfriend within six months of the restaurant opening when she refused to put up with his long hours. 'It was tough but it was inevitable,' he explains. 'In this job you have to be a little selfish. I can't take three nights off a week to sit with her or take her out to dinner. I can't be anywhere else but in my restaurant.'

Even on the very rare nights when he was elsewhere, he was worried sick. One of his business partners wanted to take him on a trip to America for the Italy versus Brazil World Cup Final in 1994, but Gordon only agreed to go if he could fly to LA and back in a day. 'It was great but I couldn't really settle,' he says. 'The whole time I was nervous about what was happening back in London.'

And, by the end of that year, Gordon had a lot more than just Aubergine to worry about. Always a man in a hurry, he was ready to sign a host of other deals to make his name, build his empire and earn some cash. One restaurant had never seemed enough for his heroes like Marco Pierre White, the Roux brothers, Raymond Blanc, Jean-Christophe Novelli and Nico Ladenis. So it wouldn't be enough for him either.

Over the next few years, Gordon entered a series of deals with other restaurants and restaurant groups. He agreed to rewrite the menus for Michael Caine's restaurant, the Canteen. The company which had helped put up the money for Aubergine was also expanding and wanted his input into its other projects. One of them was the reopening of the old Overton's restaurant in St James's Street as L'Oranger. Gordon took on a management role there as executive chef while asking his old Le Gavroche colleague Marcus Wareing to come back from Paris to be head chef.

Finally, as Britain's newfound love affair with celebrities gathered pace, Gordon joined forces with another ex-footballer, former Leeds United star Lee Chapman. Lee and his actress wife, Leslie Ash, were moving into the restaurant business and planned to set up a celebrity-friendly restaurant and club called Teatro in the heart of Soho. They wanted Gordon, as executive head chef, to help draw up the menus and set the standards that the kitchen team should follow.

Once more, Gordon got on the phone to try to arrange things. He asked Stuart Gillies, another of his former colleagues and proteges, to take charge of the brand-new £130,000 kitchen being built in an old office block behind the Palace Theatre. In total, 16 kitchen staff were recruited for Teatro – all of whom had been tested out at one of Gordon's other restaurants over the past few months.

At first, all went well at the new venture. An unlikely list of guests ranging from Geri Halliwell and Robbie Williams to Chancellor Gordon Brown came to eat and be seen at the club. But, behind the scenes, storms were brewing. Reports of Lee's lifestyle and the relationship with his wife were regularly featured in the media and Gordon was not impressed. He decided that whatever the financial cost he had to cut all ties with both Lee and Teatro.

When reporters asked him about the split, he told the *Daily Mirror*. 'There were all sorts of things happening late at night which were just beyond belief. I've witnessed all the screaming and shouting. I saw some pretty horrific things I don't wish to go into because it's not pleasant for anyone, but it's pretty low. The embarrassing nights were when Leslie was at home with the children and on the phone looking for Lee, and Lee was asking myself and head chef Stuart to lie for him and say that he's not there. But he was upstairs trying to chat up some bird. Leslie's the most endearing woman and so down-to-earth. She deserves a knighthood to put up with that kind of crap from him.

'At Teatro, I always hung around out of respect for Leslie because he's a big guy. I remember seeing him at four in the morning, abusing the staff. He pushes the self-destruct button because of his ego.' While accepting that it's okay to have a drink in the kitchen, Gordon pointed out that their need to draw a line if you want to run things smoothly.

Moving on from Teatro wasn't as easy as Gordon had hoped, however, and immediately after he dissolved the business partnership he bumped into Lee in the street – literally. 'One night, on my way from Oxford Circus I went on to Old Compton Street and bang – there he was. Lee kept blocking my path. Eventually, I had to stop a police car and ask them to intervene so that I could get on to my next appointment.' Over the next few years Chapman's mood did not change. In 1997, he was charged with common assault after a row that left Leslie with a black eye and facial bruising. She took out a restraining order against him after he followed her to the home of fellow actress Caroline Quentin. Then, in 2004, Leslie ended up in hospital after suffering injuries that both sides said had been sustained during a bout of 'rough sex'.

Back at Aubergine, the news was much, much better. Within 12 months of opening, the restaurant wasn't just making money – it was winning awards. First came the news that Gordon was being named 'Newcomer of the Year' by *Caterer and Hotelkeeper* magazine – which is a lot more important than it sounds. Winning a 'Catey' is seen as the restaurant business equivalent of getting an Oscar. And in a year with tough competition Gordon had apparently won his by a mile. 'His was simply the most stunning meal I have had in the past 12 months,' said judge David Young, an area manager for AA Hotel Division who practically ate out for a living.

Aubergine itself got some great press at the same time. 'Unlike some new ventures which peak early and then fail to get any better, the judges felt that Ramsay was still improving. He is not someone who is just sitting tight and marking time,' said fellow 'Cateys' judge Michael Raffael. And there was even better news to come. Gordon had always said that, if he couldn't get an FA Cup Winners' medal from football, he wanted to collect some Michelin stars for his cooking. With Aubergine he got one. Then another.

Michelin stars continue to be the gold standard for chefs and they are the holy grail for newcomers like Gordon wanting to make their names. Printed in secrecy each December and released every January, Michelin's restaurant guide has been going for 105 years – and has been entirely independent and unbiased for each of them. Restaurants are visited by totally anonymous inspectors who turn up or book tables like any other customer and pay their bills in full without saying who they are. There are no favours, no freebies and no clues about who is doing the judging or when a restaurant is being scrutinised. What inspectors do offer is experience. They each visit an average of 240 restaurants a year (and sleep in around 130 hotels) and any restaurant can receive up to 12 random checks in any given year before it is rated.

Input and opinions from Michelin's readers can also be taken into account before a restaurant is graded, with the next wave of inspectors told to check up on any areas which are giving others concern. 'The mystery of Michelin is what makes it so important,' says Gordon. 'You don't know the criteria that have been set, what the inspectors are looking for or when. That's why every December is hell in every kitchen in Britain. We all go through a nightmare of guesswork and gossip trying to work out who will be in and out of the next guide.'

Of the several hundred thousand restaurants in Britain, fewer than two dozen are awarded a first Michelin star each year – and they know it can be taken away at any time if their standards slip. Even fewer restaurants gain a second star, which shows the food, the service and the overall feel of the room has reached another level. At the very top of the tree is a tiny band of chefs whose restaurants have been deemed the very best in the world – these are the illustrious holders of three Michelin stars.

No one knows when or how often Gordon Ramsay's Aubergine was visited by Michelin inspectors. But, within 18 months of opening his doors, Gordon found out that their verdict on him was good. That first vital star was awarded in January 1995, when he was just 28. Over the next two years, the cooking and the overall standards at Aubergine would not just hold steady but actually improved, and the second star was awarded in 1997.

By then the great and the good were flocking to find out what was going on. Celebrities in particular had fallen in love with the restaurant and its increasingly high-profile chef – though Gordon couldn't always be bothered to ingratiate himself with them. Princess Margaret, David Bowie, Sean Connery and Robert De Niro all became regulars, while Madonna learned that Gordon was far from star-struck. She wanted a table for ten one night for dinner. She didn't get one. 'My largest table is for six and I don't care who the fuck she is, we don't do tables for ten,' he told his assistant. 'Her PA then asked if I would go to the Lanesborough Hotel [at Hyde Park Corner] and cook in her suite for £5,000 and I said no, because I'm not a prostitute.'

Gordon also admits that he might not have bothered to introduce himself even if Madonna had cut down her guest list and booked the table for six – because he rarely ventures out of the kitchen during service. He had a kitchen team of just seven at Aubergine, low by London restaurant standards, and he demanded to see every plate that was produced before the waiters took it to a customer. He also wanted to see every plate coming back after a meal, to check exactly what had and hadn't been eaten. It left no time to play mine host in the dining room – which was just how Gordon liked it. 'I'm not a smarmy-arse. I don't think you should walk into the dining room and grace tables, standing there like some starched stiff erection, gawping at customers and asking how the food was, going round shaking hands. I've never done that, and I can't suck up to people.'

The confidence that his food could do his talking was what kept Gordon going through all the early mornings, the late nights and the endless stress of running his own business. He was paying himself around £24,000 a year, substantially less than his maitre d' was earning, so that he could plough as much as possible back into the restaurant. Friends say he worried constantly about money and was always doing sums to check his finances remained sound. For example, after spending an essential £7,000 revarnishing the restaurant floor, he sat and worked out how many plates of lobster ravioli and other dishes he would have to sell to recoup the money.

But towards the end of 1997 Gordon was finally allowing himself to believe that he could recoup it – and more. Aubergine had survived the curse of 11 Park Walk and was turning into one of London's 'must visit' restaurants alongside those of all the more established master chefs. His name was becoming known alongside those of all his heroes in the industry, and after each exhausting 18-hour day he felt closer to his ultimate goal of winning three Michelin stars. Back then, it really did look as if his life and his business would be a success. It looked as if being forced out of Rangers and taking the plunge back into catering had been the right move.

As the months passed and the accolades mounted up, Gordon decided he might even get back in touch with his father to see if he might finally get the parental approval he still craved. Looking back, Gordon says that for the first time in his life he pretty much allowed himself to relax. Which was precisely when he got his first death threat.

should head to Paris. Armed with some letters of recommendation, Gordon did just that. At that point, Paris was still the world's most renowned culinary capital. It was where the giants of the art worked. And it was going to change Gordon's life.

His first job was at the world-famous Guy Savoy restaurant. But before it began Gordon had time for his first-ever working holiday. He headed south to the ski resort of Isola 2000 in Provence, where he was to live and work at the Hotel Diva. 'I was at work at 7.30 in the morning to set up service. Then I'd ski from midday till 4pm, then be back in the kitchen from 5.30pm until midnight.' Little did he know back then that these would be the shortest working hours he would experience for some time.

Back in Paris, Gordon started to learn more about cooking, as well as more about himself. 'You can never be bored in Paris. It's a boisterous place and a rude city and the Parisians are incredibly arrogant. I think it is a place that helped to form my character. I found out a lot about myself in Paris and I think I found my soul there.' He also found a French girlfriend, a tall, dark-haired Parisian who was a waitress at the prestigious George V Hotel. And he found professional inspiration in the elegant and intimate surroundings of the Guy Savoy.

'One of the many things Guy taught me is that flavour is the most important aspect of a dish,' Gordon says. 'I trained my palate in Paris and learned that taste is what should be held in the memory, not what the dish looks like on the plate for the first 30 seconds. People pay big money for food which tastes phenomenal, not just for something

FOUR

DEATH THREATS

'If you know what's good for you, you want to check underneath your car before starting the engine.' The chilling words came in a letter sent to Gordon at Aubergine early in 1998. They were just one of many threats made that spring. Other letters warned him of an arson attack, of late-night beatings on his way home from the restaurant, and of death.

The police were called and it turned out there was more than just the anonymous letters to investigate. A Range Rover had been parked outside the restaurant for two hours the previous Friday and when the dinner service had begun someone had climbed out of the passenger seat, walked calmly up to the front desk, grabbed the reservations book and run back to the car. With the engine already running, the Range Rover had soon disappeared in the early evening traffic.

Gordon's first thought was that a rival in the industry was hoping to sabotage his business. But it turned out to be a lot more twisted than that. Taking a reservations book in the pre-computer age was a massive blow to a popular, expensive restaurant such as Aubergine. It was where the names and contact details of every booking for up to six months ahead were stored. Without the book, a restaurant had no way of knowing who or how many people would be arriving on any given night. They couldn't confirm any bookings or confidently make any new ones. 'Only someone in the trade would know the full true value of a reservations book,' Gordon told reporter Christina Golding after the theft. Only a rival would know that what they had stolen was worth its weight in gold.

But would a rival want to twist the knife by faxing Gordon the previous night's pages every morning? And would they go to the trouble of doing so from a different print shop in London every day? It was when these faxes were being sent that the first set of letters began to arrive. And with them came defaced copies of magazine articles about Gordon, covered in obscene drawings and gruesome requests for a table for two.

The police never found out who had stolen the reservations book or sent the obscene letters. It could have been a rival, it could have been an unhappy diner, it could have been a madman – no one knows. So Gordon and his staff just tried to carry on as normal, juggling bookings and squeezing in and serving any extra diners who turned up in the confusion. 'Just forget it,' Gordon was told when the police investigation finally wound down. 'Put it behind you and try and move on. Focus on better things.'

And fortunately, after years of being single and putting up with some unsatisfying short-term relationships, Gordon did have something good to focus on. Her name was Cayetana Hutcheson and she was a trainee teacher who was working part-time as an assistant manageress at Terence Conran's famous Le Pont de la Tour restaurant beside Tower Bridge. Cayetana, whom everyone called Tana, was just 18. She was pretty. She was funny. She was confident. And she was engaged to Gordon's best friend.

The trio, Tim, Tana and Gordon, would meet up on the banks of the Thames outside Le Pont de la Tour in the early hours after their shifts had ended. They would sit and gaze at Tower Bridge, watch the traditional Thames barges drift by and talk about kitchens, cooking and customers. They would also meet at Tim's flat, where Gordon often stored his Yamaha FZR motorbike. And Gordon grew more and more determined to see Tana on her own.

At first glance, they didn't seem to have a huge amount in common. Tana had been born and brought up in a tiny village in leafy Kent, a far cry from Gordon's council estates in Glasgow and Stratford. She had become a weekly boarder at a private prep school in suburban Dulwich before the family had moved further into London and she had switched to a secondary school in Holland Park. She had a full-time mother and her father, Christopher, ran a successful print company. Hers was a close-knit family – her parents had stayed together and she had two brothers and a sister to complement Gordon's two sisters and a brother. But, for all the differences in their backgrounds, both Gordon and Tana say there was an obvious spark between them from the very start. And, luckily for Gordon, the spark between Tana and Tim was fading.

'I think the relationship had run its course and it was just a question of making a bit of an effort to get out of it,' Tana says of the way her engagement finally ended.

Gordon and his motorbike were to provide the impetus. 'One night, I phoned up and Tana sounded upset about something and I said, "Well, I'm coming to pick my bike up," and we ended up going for a ride through London at 2.30am in the middle of summer. It was fantastic and I've never forgotten it. That night was when we knew something was going to happen between us,' says Gordon.

Tana admits she needed a tiny bit more persuading. 'First of all, he drove me mad because he kept going on about our age difference. But I was flattered by his attention and pretty quickly I was certain that I wanted to be with him. He had this aura from the start. I loved his passion, his dedication and his determination,' she says. 'He just struck me as being so ambitious and driven.' The respect seemed to be mutual. 'I was working at Le Pont de la Tour to supplement my income while I was training to be a teacher and I think he admired that about me as well.'

The couple's early dates were not easy, though, because they were both working long hours and were rarely free either in the day or in the evenings. 'So what happened was Gordon would pick me up from work on his motorbike and maybe drive out to Banbury. We'd sit by a river there and talk for hours. Later, when he had moved to London, we would meet at 2am after he finished work and go to a club or find a place for late drinks. We'd then be up the next morning for work at 6am. It was exhausting but exhilarating. Looking back, it's amazing that we made it work, but we did. The relationship was exciting and we inspired each other and there was always a strong chemistry between us. We had some wild times and lots of fun. But very little sleep.'

With everything falling into place both at work and at home, Gordon felt ready for even more challenges. Being with Tana energised him, he says, and restored his faith in good relationships. This was particularly important to him back then, as his previous short-term relationship hadn't ended particularly well. While saying he has never done anything untoward with an annoying customer's food, he admitted he had 'tampered with' vinaigrette he made for his girlfriend after a row. She left him, and six months later came out as a lesbian. He never found out if the two events were connected.

Desperately hoping history wouldn't repeat itself with Tana, Gordon was also desperate to cram even more hours into the day. He had signed a deal to write his first book, hoping it could improve his reputation, force him to research even more recipes and, perhaps most importantly, earn enough money to clear some of his debts.

A Passion for Flavour turned out to do all three, though the book wasn't universally liked by critics or readers. Gordon had put a hundred recipes in it, including those for soups, starters, fish and meat dishes and desserts. He adapted several of Aubergine's most popular dishes so that people could make them at home. But he refused to compromise on either the ingredients readers were supposed to use or the effort they were supposed to put into their work. 'It's essentially a restaurant manual rather than a home cookbook and it's certainly not for the beginner,' said one early reviewer, not that keen on the idea of tackling a steak dish that took two days to prepare.

'Gordon Ramsay appears to be a serious chef and he seems to expect the same from his readers,' wrote another. 'There are precious few shortcuts in these recipes and you may sometimes feel you are being told what to do rather than being helped.'

'The pictures are nice and glossy but what use are all the recipes for posh nosh like pheasant and quails' eggs and asparagus? Where does he think we are going to get that kind of stuff? Down at the local Spar?' asked another unhappy reader.

Despite the criticism, the book won the Glenfiddich Award as Food Book of the Year and that gave Gordon enough confidence to break the habit of a lifetime and take a holiday. He was going to leave Aubergine, the other restaurants and all his business affairs behind for a couple of days and go away with Tana. He had a question for her.

For her part, Tana had a feeling about what was coming. 'Everything had changed for both of us when we had started going out and I think we both very quickly knew that this was it. There was no point in hanging around.' So, in the South of France, Gordon proposed. Tana admits it was hardly the most romantic of events. 'He just said, "It's such a nice relationship. Let's get married." I said "Yes" straight away.'

Neither wanted a long engagement and they set a date just five months ahead. On the big day, Tana was just 21 while Gordon was 29. The ceremony took place in a tiny church in Chelsea and they were then driven over to the

Cafe Royal in Regent Street for the reception. 'It was the last Saturday before Christmas, it was cold and frosty, all the lights were up and all the shoppers stopped to look when the wedding cars arrived,' recalls Tana. 'The whole thing was just magical.'

Married life, however, was not exactly conventional. They had moved into a top-floor loft apartment in a converted school building in far from glamorous Stockwell, in south London. There, in the couple's bedroom, sat a giant stuffed frog. 'Did that used to belong to one of you as a child?' a friend once asked Tana when he saw it. 'No,' she replied. 'It's Gordon's. He bought it on our honeymoon.' And, having proved himself to be one of the least romantic men around, Gordon said that while he and Tana spoke on the phone several times every day they hardly ever saw each other during the week. And he admits that he would frequently fall asleep on their Sunday dates at the cinema or in rival restaurants.

'Tana is so patient, she understands that I have to put my life on hold for this,' he said when asked about how married life fitted in with the demands of Aubergine and his other businesses. 'I have no social life, really, but I am building for our future together.'

What he didn't know back then was that within little more than a year that future would be on the edge of collapse. At 31, he had achieved so much. And it suddenly looked as if he was going to throw it all away.

FIVE

STARTING AGAIN

The crunch came in early 1998 when Gordon Ramsay and Aubergine were firmly established as serious players on the London restaurant scene. Both the man and the restaurant were seen as potential money-makers. And people were lining up to get a piece of them. Gordon was being swamped with job offers, business propositions and promotional opportunities. As a hot young chef, he could put his name to anything from pots and pans to frozen peas. He knew he could cash in, spread himself as thinly as required and make as much money as he could in the shortest possible time.

Or he could play the long game. He could continue to develop his craft. He could become more professional, more disciplined, more demanding. He could win that third Michelin star before his 33rd birthday, setting a new record in the process. He was convinced that if he stayed focused he could become one of the greatest and most influential chefs in the world. But, just as Gordon decided that this was the route he should take, everyone else tried to persuade him differently. Desperate though he was to stay in the kitchen, his bosses and backers all seemed to want him in the boardroom.

When Marco Pierre White bowed out of Aubergine after helping Gordon raise the funds he required to set it up, a private company became one of the largest shareholders in the venture. It was A-Z Restaurants, a mainly Italian-owned catering company, and for years everyone was happy with the way Gordon's business was being run. The money men could hardly complain about their chef's level of commitment or his award-winning professional achievements. But A-Z Restaurants had expansion plans that threatened to change everything.

The bosses had decided that the international restaurant scene was ripe for rationalisation. They felt a single winning formula could be created and relaunched in a series of different locations. If the company didn't get the funds for this sort of venture from a new partner, there was a plan to float the firm on the stock exchange. Either way, it looked like a chain of Ramsay-inspired eateries was on the cards. There was talk of Aubergine Paris, Aubergine New York and Aubergine Bermuda being rolled out. Even a range of Aubergine Pizzerias for British high streets. Gordon, not surprisingly, was horrified.

'I would have had to replicate everything at Aubergine as a concept in catering,' he said. 'But restaurants of this nature are personal, not concept. My choice was to be an individual. I don't want to produce clones.' To do so could have made him rich. At one point, a potential partner came forward with an offer to buy out the company's current owners, valuing Gordon's stake in the firm at £1.5 million. In cash.

But the man who had been forced to ask a charity for help when he needed to buy chef's knives and whites for his college course says money was the last thing to motivate him. Fed up with spending so much time in business meetings with A-Z's owners, he resigned as a director of the company while he looked around to see if he might prefer to run another restaurant elsewhere – though he had no intention of leaving his treasured Aubergine. Or at least he hadn't until he saw how much pressure his friend and colleague Marcus Wareing seemed to be under at L'Oranger.

The company wanted Marcus to sign a four-year contract there to reassure potential investors about the company's medium-term stability. But Marcus wasn't keen on the direction the company was taking either, so he refused. At which point, he says, he was sacked. Gordon resigned in protest and all hell broke loose.

During Gordon's contractual week-long notice period, his staff at both Aubergine and L'Oranger were horrified at what was going on. Far from living in fear with what ITV had called 'Britain's worst boss', they were in fact hugely supportive of the chef who had taught, given and inspired them so much. They wanted to stay with him. So, when Gordon finally walked through the restaurant's doors for the last time, an extraordinary 46 of them joined him. 'Overnight, Ramsay has effectively closed down two of London's most celebrated restaurants,' wrote *Times* journalist Susan Chenery. They stayed closed for several weeks as the owners tried to recruit new workers, and customers decided that if neither Gordon nor Marcus was going to be in the kitchens they didn't want to hold on to their bookings.

For Gordon, these were tense, difficult weeks. He felt a huge responsibility to the 46 staff who had left good jobs to support him – and who wouldn't be able to last long without a replacement wage. But what could he do next? Psychologists say that in times of crisis people tend to think big or think small. Those who think small batten down the hatches, look for the safest options and lick their wounds in private. People who think big decide that if life has messed everything up they might as well make one more gamble and to hell with the consequences. Gordon was thinking big. Aubergine had been a fantastic opportunity and he had made it work. He knew he could do it again. But this time he wanted a place with his own name above the door.

Marcus joined him as he continued to scour London for ideas, possible premises and generous partners. What inspired them the most was the site of a famous but recently closed restaurant, La Tante Claire, in Royal Hospital Road, Chelsea. La Tante Claire had enjoyed a glorious 21-year history and won three Michelin stars under chef Pierre Koffman before being moved to new premises in the Berkeley Hotel in Knightsbridge. French-born Pierre was frequently called 'the chef's chef' and tended to come top of the list when professionals were asked to pick their dream kitchen team for a fantasy restaurant. He, his restaurant and his reputation would be a hard act to follow. But Gordon and Marcus decided to go for it. They would do whatever it took to buy the site, go hell for leather to get it ready and reopen very soon under a new name: Gordon Ramsay's name.

Raising the money for a venture like this was the first major challenge and both Gordon and Tana were prepared to gamble everything they had on its success. Every penny of their joint savings went into the fighting fund and they got a group of estate agents round to value their flat. Picking the keenest-looking of the bunch, Gordon told him to sell it as fast as possible to provide even more ready cash. He and Tana had agreed they would go back to renting for as long as it took to get the new restaurant off the ground. Meanwhile, Tana's dad, Chris, got on the phone to find other backers and helped set up a massive loan from Bank of Scotland.

From the very start, a huge amount of money and hope was going to be riding on this deal – and the pressure started to show straight away. Within months of trying to secure the premises and the finance, Gordon went from 15 to 17 stone as comfort eating and lack of exercise took their toll. 'I let myself go because I was totally possessed and totally obsessed with getting the place right,' he says.

Once he had got the keys to the old La Tante Claire building, almost £250,000 was spent on the refit, and among other items used to decorate the rooms were mirrors and ornaments he and Tana had found on trips to New York and Venice. Those people who today dismiss the man as a television star rather than a genuine restaurateur need only look back at the kitchen work he did then to see just how wrong they are. Obsessed by creating a newer, better menu, the former footballer threw himself into the intricacies of food. He went back to basics in the early hours, recreating purees, sauces and soups so that his next menu would be uniquely his. The man brought up on egg and chips was putting 'pot au feu of pigeon served in a cepe bouillon with chou farci' through its paces until it tasted as good as it looked.

'Gordon is obsessed and he can – and does – talk about a simple cooking stock such as vegetable *nage* for hours on end,' said food expert Thane Prince, who watched Gordon at work on his new recipes. She, and everyone else, also saw Gordon's extreme impatience as the opening night of the restaurant named after him approached. 'I am incredibly excited, the feeling I have for this place is just massive and I just want to look forward now, to get in my kitchen, shut the door and concentrate,' he said with days to go.

But, when the big moment came, it all very nearly ended in disaster. 'We had 52 people in the restaurant and the air-conditioning went down in the kitchen. I just couldn't afford to close. So we had to cook in temperatures of 150 degrees – people were dropping like flies. It was absolutely horrendous, one of the worst nights of my entire life,' he said later. But it was also a personal and a professional triumph.

The big gamble had paid off. Gordon Ramsay the restaurant was attracting all the customers who had been loyal to the chef for the past five years. People wanted to be seen there and, with the air-conditioning working again, Gordon could focus on new menus to surprise them.

Meanwhile, things were not going so well back at Aubergine and L'Oranger. At one point, it was reported that the owners were losing £15,000 a week by keeping them closed while they tried to recover from seeing Gordon and Marcus disappear. When they reopened a month later, after cancelling an unprecedented three months of future bookings, the owners said takings never approached their former highs. The magic and the loyal, high-spending customers had gone. Someone had to pay for it and it looked as if that someone was going to be Gordon.

A High Court writ arrived on his desk early the following year. He was being sued for an estimated £1.5 million and his reputation was about to take a battering. As well as complaining about the financial losses, A-Z Restaurants had some other allegations to make. Most shocking was that Gordon and Marcus had made a 'night-time raid' on L'Oranger the day after Marcus had been sacked – and that in the course of it they did £30,000 worth of damage. As well as sabotage and theft, Gordon in particular was accused of breaking the terms of his old employment contract by ringing up some of the group's key staff and asking them to resign alongside him.

'Every aspect of this case will be contested all the way,' Gordon declared from his new restaurant when news of the massive writ broke. But he never got his day in court. Just before the hearing was to begin, both sides agreed to settle their differences – on terms that have never been revealed. 'I can't go into great detail because every time I mention it I get inundated with horses' heads on the doorstep,' Gordon joked afterwards about the agreement he had made with his former bosses. Anyway, by this point he had several other, more pressing events to deal with. One of them was good, one of them was bad and one would take his life in an entirely new direction.

The good news was the birth of his first daughter, Megan, which took place while Gordon was a long way from the maternity ward – of which a lot more later. But, as he and Tana had wanted to start a family as soon as possible after getting married, he was over the moon to be a father so quickly. And he was determined to make a better job of it than his own dad had.

Gordon senior, who had disappeared to Spain nearly a decade earlier, had only rarely been heard from since. Gordon's mother, Helen, had remarried, and Gordon says her new husband, Jimmy, had proved to be a better man from day one. It was obvious by 1998 that the Ramsay family was getting on just fine without any echoes from the past. But, having just become a father himself, Gordon found he could no longer stop thinking about his own father, and of what might have been.

'I began to long for him to meet Tana and Megan and I kept wondering what he would make of it all. Would he at last admit his son was a success – even in a profession for which he had no respect? I knew I wanted to hear him say just once, "Well done, son, you've done great. You made the right decision all those years ago. Who needs football?" But I was giving up hope of ever having that conversation.' Until one day, out of the blue, it looked as if all those wishes might be granted.

'I suddenly got a call from Dad asking to see me – he was back in England to see a doctor and was staying in Margate in Kent.' They arranged to meet up the following week, but when Gordon arrived he could hardly recognise the old man standing in front of him. 'I was shocked at how much older and frailer he looked. He was in such a pitiable state that I felt more sorrow for him than anger. We went for a walk along the pier and I told him that he had to sort himself out and try and make a living for himself. He was 53 years old, was effectively living out of the back of a van and owned nothing in the whole world.'

Trying to recreate the past, the pair went to a cafe by the pier for a full English breakfast. And straight away the old tensions began to show. 'I asked for toast instead of fried bread and Dad told me not to be such a snob. I tried to tell him about the kind of fat that places used for fried bread but he wasn't interested. We were in different worlds.' But father and son still parted as close to being friends as they had been since the days they had sat quietly fishing on the banks of the Tay.

'It was as if we had resolved something that day. Finally, we had begun to feel close again,' says Gordon. 'I gave him £1,000 to put a deposit down on a flat to rent and we arranged that he would come to London the following month, not only to meet Tana and his grandchild but also to eat for the first time at my restaurant. The last thing I remember is looking back after we had said goodbye and feeling sorry for him. He was staring after me, crying.'

The big day when Gordon senior was due to arrive was set for 25 January 1999 and Gordon says he was as thrilled and excited about it as a child waiting for Christmas. 'I just wanted to see him sitting at the table with a smile on his face. Even if he had sat there and got pissed I would have forgiven him.'

But it was never to be. Gordon senior had a massive heart attack on New Year's Eve and died within 24 hours. Anger and frustration bubbles up in his son's mind to this day. 'No one should die at just 53. I am so angry at him for dying so young and for not looking after himself. And I couldn't believe I would never now get the fatherly seal of approval I so longed for. I had managed to have that one frank talk with him in Margate before he died. But I really wanted to ask him much more. Was he relieved about what I had done? Was he proud? I never got the chance. I got the feeling of unfinished business that will probably be with me for the rest of my life.'

Gordon remembers helping carry his father's coffin into the church on the day of his funeral. 'Stay strong, stay strong, stay strong,' he mumbled to himself as the whole family suffered with the mixed emotions of guilt, anger, loss, love and, perhaps, relief.

When 25 January came, the table for two where Gordon's dad and his new girlfriend were to have eaten sat empty as a silent tribute to the man Gordon had both loved and feared, respected and despised.

As well as never getting to meet Tana or Megan or eat his son's food, Gordon senior was also to miss the other event which was to reshape Gordon's life that spring: his debut on national television. A production company had approached him more than a year earlier about a project they had been planning for some time. Inspired by an explosion of interest in cooking, the company wanted to show what really happened inside a high-pressure, high-class commercial kitchen. They wanted fly-on-the-wall cameras to follow the life of a personable, charismatic, possibly even volatile chef to show diners what was really happening on the other side of the kitchen doors.

But which chef to choose? Marco Pierre White was one

obvious choice as his own roots in a broken home in Leeds gave him the street cred that the producers were looking for. Some of the older names were also in the frame, though the aim was to introduce viewers to a new generation of chefs rather than rely on those from the past. The likes of Gary Rhodes, Rick Stein and the heart-throb Jean-Christophe Novelli also went under the microscope.

But it was only when the producers first heard about Gordon that they knew they had hit the jackpot. Back then, he had won his first batch of awards and was desperately hungry for more. He was the ex-professional footballer, the boy from the ugly Glasgow council estate who was making some of the most exquisite food in London. And he was under a hell of a lot of pressure.

When the producers first came over to discuss the project, Gordon was still at Aubergine in Fulham. It was booming, but Gordon was still having sleepless nights about the money everyone had borrowed to set it up, and about the famously fickle restaurant trade. Celebrities and every other type of diner were keeping the tables filled for every lunch and dinner service. But Gordon knew there were no guarantees that a rival restaurant wouldn't make some headlines and steal them all away overnight.

Friends and colleagues said Gordon was crazy to let the cameras in on his life. But at 31 he thought he had no choice. Any publicity was good publicity, he believed. So he signed on the dotted line. His life was going to be public property like never before.

Channel 4 was overjoyed. 'We chose Gordon because he's the best chef in Britain and because he makes great television,' a spokesman told the *Mail on Sunday* just before the series was aired. What they had loved most about him during filming was that he was the classic good-looking, angry young man, full of passion, contradictions and surprises – a genius chef with hooligan tendencies. Better still, he didn't care if all of it was captured on camera.

When the show's producers looked at the early tapes, they knew straight away what the series should be called: *Boiling Point*. Shown over nearly two months, it covered Gordon's final days at Aubergine as well as the high-stress opening of Gordon Ramsay in Chelsea. As promised, it also opened the door on the reality of life in a kitchen and on the take-no-prisoners style of this particular chef. Gordon was shown yelling and swearing viciously at almost every member of his kitchen team from the moment the opening credits had ended. 'Episode One ended with an employee cycling away in tears after being fired, Ramsay muttering: "I don't give a shit," as he went. For Episode Three, a special occasion in which the president of Michelin visited the restaurant, Ramsay rose to the occasion and wheeled out the c-word,' was how one newspaper summed it up.

Throw in some gratuitous insults of the people who supplied the restaurant with food, Gordon's extraordinary fury when he found out a turbot had been overcooked by 30 seconds and his relentless demands for better work, and a television phenomenon was born. 'Every dish, every meal, every day has to be perfection' became Gordon's mantra on the show – repeated endlessly and with an ever-increasing choice of key adjectives in almost every episode. 'Is your brain in your fucking arse, you fucking fat bastard?' he had screamed, to give one example from the first show.

'You're going to lose your job, dick-head,' he crowed in the next. 'What about opening your big French eyes, arsehole?' he roared, rounding things off nicely.

What also made headlines was Gordon's uncompromising attitude to the food his staff were creating. Any imperfections and it was thrown back at them – sometimes literally. Whole platefuls, and often the plates themselves, were flung into the bin every evening. It was like no kitchen viewers had ever seen before.

'The man is clearly an ogre and rarely has television witnessed anybody being so vile to their staff,' said one reviewer.

Others found they had an even stronger reaction. 'Shortly after watching *Boiling Point*, about Britain's most brilliant and furious young chef, I had to go out for a walk, just to cool down. I was seething with directionless rage, catching it off Ramsay, whose profanities tumble out of his gob in a hailstorm of abuse, firing off invective which seems to be both deeply personal and yet random, as if the whole world needs bollocking all the time,' wrote Charles Jennings, television reviewer of the *Observer*.

And readers of the tabloids were getting pretty much the same message – though in shorter words they could tailor to their own purposes. Gordon says a group of brickies, scaffolders and other workmen taking their lunch breaks on London's Tottenham Court Road took to shouting: 'Table Nine, you fucking arsehole!' whenever they saw him heading down the road to work, for example.

Long famous for his four-course meals, Gordon had a new trademark: his liberal use of four-letter words. He tried to laugh off the criticism, saying he was using the language of the industry and had nothing to apologise for. But not everyone agreed.

Viewers had flooded the broadcasting watchdog the Independent Television Commission with complaints about both the language and the events in *Boiling Point*. Gordon's 'persistent use of the f-word' triggered most of the complaints but, as the ITC explained, 'Some viewers also felt that scenes in which he bullied his staff and indulged in unhygienic kitchen practices gave the impression that such behaviour was acceptable.'

The complaint about strong language was the first to be rejected, however. Attempts by Channel 4 to bleep out the worst of the language had not worked, the report said, because 'Strong language was indivisible from Ramsay's excitable and aggressive persona at work'. The ITV ruled that Channel 4's strong warning about what was to come at the start of each show should have alerted any sensitive viewers. It also dismissed the broader complaints about what went on in Gordon's kitchens because 'No encouragement was given to regard Ramsay's behaviour as normal or acceptable'.

While some may have seen a statement such as this as a pretty strong insult, Gordon said he was just pleased to be able to carry on as before. But, before he could do so, he had to face some fire from his peers. David Wood, chief executive of the Hotel and Catering International Management Association, said the ITC wasn't the only organisation being inundated with complaints about Gordon's onscreen antics. 'I am getting phone calls from parents saying their children are no longer going to become chefs,' he said. 'There are so many positive portrayals of chefs but Ramsay pushes it all down the pan. I wish he were still in football. Then we could send him off.'

Anne Walker, managing director of catering recruitment company Springboard UK, said, 'At a college last week, students were saying that they were so horrified by what they had seen that they were no longer sure that this was the kind of industry they wanted to go into.'

After dealing with Gordon, some existing workers found they couldn't get out of the industry fast enough. In fact, in the summer of 1999, Gordon was actually arrested for allegedly beating up one of his staff – 22-year-old pastry chef Nathan Thomas. The row, of all things, had begun over the shape of a banana parfait.

'Ramsay kept going on about it not being ball-shaped enough,' Nathan told the police. 'He just went berserk. When I said I was quitting, he went mad, telling me I was ungrateful. He's a bully. A genius, but a monster.'

Police confirmed the arrest and Ramsay was bailed to appear at Chelsea police station the following month. Fortunately, by then, all sides had accepted that it was a storm in a restaurant teacup and the case, with all charges, was dropped. Gordon's tough-guy reputation, however, had moved up another gear.

One final person was ready to speak out against the way Gordon was acting and the language he was using in 1999: his mother Helen. 'She rang me up and told me that my language is appalling. I said, "Mum, you should have been sat in the dressing room at Rangers when we were losing 2–0." When I'm working I get upset and I tried to explain that to her. All I am using is the language you hear in every kitchen and she does seem to accept that. Everyone swears in kitchens if they want to produce the best food. If a kitchen is silent and everyone says "please" and "thank you", then you'd never hit the heights. I'm focused on producing the best and, if swearing makes that happen, then I'll keep on doing it.'

The good news for Gordon was that his diners seemed to like the fact that their food was being prepared with passion. As its popularity grew, the restaurant became a fixture of the gossip columns and saw a near-endless stream of famous names pass through the doors, sometimes a little worse for wear from drink. And the rest of the world had also started to wake up to the Gordon Ramsay phenomenon – though the man himself continued to take it all in his stride.

'There was one American critic who demanded a free meal for a review and said she could only come at 8.30pm that Friday night,' he recalls. 'The restaurant was fully booked and the critic refused to accept that paying punters who may have made their plans months ahead could not be excluded just to make room for her and her companion.'

In the end, Gordon said he could offer the critic the table she wanted at 8.30pm on the Saturday night instead. What he 'forgot' to tell her was that Gordon Ramsay didn't open on Saturday nights. 'It was wicked, I know,' he says. 'I wanted to drive round in a car with tinted windows to see what happened when she turned up.'

This fearless attitude to critics, opinion-formers, celebrities and all the other people that chefs normally suck up to was yet another way Gordon drew himself apart from his peers. It had always been part of his personality; now it had become part of his appeal. And it was on full display on the infamous night that Joan Collins came to dinner.

SIX

JOAN COLLINS? YOU'RE OUT

To this day, Gordon says he never intended to throw Joan Collins out of his restaurant before she had even tasted her starter. His problem, he says, was never with her. It was with the man sitting opposite her, the restaurant critic AA Gill.

Gill is easily one of the most acerbic and idiosyncratic restaurant reviewers in the business. His pieces are often hilarious – sometimes focusing almost entirely on himself, his companions and on his journeys to and from the restaurant in question, with just a brief mention of the food or the atmosphere tacked on to the end. Readers have always loved it – but restaurant owners and chefs are not always so keen.

One of Gordon's contentions was that Gill veered too far and too frequently from discussing the food or the ambience of a restaurant and ended up commenting on the one set of people Gordon saw as above approach: the customers. For someone with an ever-growing reputation as an angry, aggressive and frequently unpleasant perfectionist, Gordon always felt genuine warmth towards the paying punter, and after all it was his wish to please the customer that made him so demanding of his staff.

'One night a lady ordered the caramelised duck with a puree of dates,' he says, to illustrate his attitude towards diners. 'She asked for the duck to be well done and Jean-Claude, my manager, asked me, "How do you feel about that?" I said, "Jean-Claude, she's paying, she can have it fucking raw if she wants. I'll serve the neck if she likes and she can have the feet to take home for a consomme."'

Gordon didn't believe that AA Gill was always quite so respectful of the general public, however. 'Bloated Godalming plutocrats and their popsies' was just one unpleasant image of Gordon's typical customers recently conjured up on Gill's keyboard. In a bid to stop things escalating and provoking more verbal attacks, Gordon went over to the critic one night when they were both eating at the Ivy, in London's theatreland. He told him that if Gill didn't stick to criticising the food and the service he would no longer be welcome at his restaurant.

That, Gordon thought, was that. The journalist thought differently. Shortly afterwards, AA Gill booked into Gordon Ramsay under an assumed name, as he always did, and took his seat with his girlfriend and the actress Joan Collins. Sensing a potential problem, the maitre d' went into the kitchen to tell Gordon who was there, and the chef came out to tackle the problem head on. He shook the critic by the hand to say hello, no voices were raised and no threats were made. He simply asked Gill and his guests to leave and they did so.

The newspapers, of course, didn't see things so simply. They went wild when they heard that Joan Collins was among the three diners ousted from the restaurant and the story even made it on to *The News at Ten*. As the affair continued to make headlines, everyone wanted their chance to explain what had really happened. And Gill was first into print, giving his side of the story in the next weekend's *Sunday Times* when he began by posing the question: 'Why should Gordon Ramsay take against me?'

'In the past, I have reviewed three restaurants he has been associated with: Aubergine, where I said the food was good, but the service and the atmosphere were shocking. Then there was L'Oranger, where he didn't cook but was executive chef. I gave that a rave review. And there was some club run by a footballer where Ramsay had lent his name to the menu, which was so-so. I pointed out that in general restaurants he didn't cook in were nicer than ones where he did (and Glasgow Rangers were doing quite well now he's not playing for them). Well, that's obviously enough. Gordon says this is personal.'

Saying that it was nothing of the sort, Gill went on to claim that in Gordon's opinion he had only brought Joan Collins along to try to stop him being thrown out. 'I understand that the concept of having friends may well be novel to Ramsay but I'm not yet reduced to touting round Hollywood for bodyguards to protect me from kitchen staff,' was his response. Now on fine form, Gill had a whole lot more to say. 'Ramsay said he was pleased it was the first restaurant I'd been thrown out of, because it was like losing your virginity, which tells you a lot about his attitude to sex,' was one of his other good lines that weekend.

But for all the humour there was a darker side to the critic's comments. Describing Gordon as 'the vastly self-important, self-regarding narcissist of the culinary world', he went on to put forward his own theory about the real reason for the night's events. 'We are looking down the maw of a recession and the restaurant business is too fat and has borrowed too much money in the belief that there would be no end to the rich suckers who will always take a table. It may well be that cold fear lay behind Gordon's tantrum. This is not a good time to have invested a huge amount of your family's money in a very small and frankly hideous restaurant in a backwater in Chelsea with no passing trade. Ramsay says it's been booked solid since he opened and is full up a month ahead. Well, we got a table, booked under a false name, that afternoon. Perhaps we were just lucky. Gordon's right to be frightened. He has a million reasons to be frightened and only 40 covers between him and a sandwich round.

'What's really so sad is that Ramsay is a very good cook. He has two well-earned Michelin stars. The cult of celebrity chef was the worst thing that could ever have happened to him. In the kitchen he's brilliant. In the dining room he's barely house-trained.'

Gordon, not surprisingly, refused to accept any of Gill's criticism – and he enjoyed a temporary bookings boost when diners rang up and specifically asked to sit at the table from which Joan and AA Gill had been ejected. On the night in question, however, Gordon claimed that Gill had been rude to the staff from the moment he had entered the restaurant. And that, alongside being rude to his customers, was utterly against Gordon's moral code.

'People said I threw him out for the publicity. Utter crap. I'm protective of my family and my staff. If it was the food he was complaining about, I would take it on the chin and say I'd fucked up. I don't mind if people criticise food, or even call me a failed footballer. But over the past two or three years he's become personal and vindictive. He's a powerful journalist and I don't think journalists should write for egotistical reasons. So I just got pissed off and threw him out. But I asked him in a very polite, well-mannered fashion. Not in an arrogant, stomping, swearing fashion. I just shook him by the hand and asked him to leave. That's all. It got blown out of all proportion.'

It did, however, get Gordon in trouble with his mum. 'Oh, Gordon, you shouldn't have put Joan out, she's such an example to ladies over 50,' Helen told him over the phone when he admitted what he had done.

But even this didn't make him change his ways or stop him speaking his mind. Months later, when Joan Collins did finally brave his restaurant a second time – without Gill at her side – Gordon was happy to serve her. But he was hardly complimentary afterwards. 'She was very white,' he said ungallantly. 'I think it was the make-up. She looked like she was performing in *The Mummy Returns*.'

Collins, for her part, was prepared to give as good as she got that night. She asked the maitre d' if Gordon was in the restaurant on the night she was there.

'Of course,' she was told. 'Would you like me to get him?'

'Oh no,' she said. 'Keep him in the kitchen, where he's best.'

Having weathered the storms from broadcasting watchdogs, the catering profession, the critics and Joan Collins, Gordon had one final challenge to address before the year was out. Of all people, a group of apple farmers from Kent had started to picket his restaurant and were threatening to take him to court.

Their problem was simple. Nine months earlier, when money was tight, Gordon had accepted £3,500 to replace Denise Van Outen as the celebrity spokesperson for British Bramley apples. As part of the deal, he had agreed to come up with a new recipe for the apples which he was to perform on television. But, when the show aired, it turned out that he had used French Granny Smiths instead – and, worse still, he had said that diners wouldn't know the difference.

'Ramsay was very quick to take our money and very quick to stab us in the back,' said Jo Rimmer, spokesman for the English Bramley Apple Growers' Association, afterwards. 'We paid him £3,500 and he said on screen that it was the easiest money he had ever earned for half an hour's work. Now we feel we have been cheated.'

Afterwards, Gordon blamed the poor quality of some of the British apples for the problem. 'I am a perfectionist and the second crate they sent was not perfect. I was left with no choice but to use the Granny Smiths.'

Unwilling to accept this, the farmers, whose chairman, Ian Mitchell, had been called 'a plonker' during the broadcast, decided to picket Gordon's restaurant. 'Down the King's Road they trekked, all these apple farmers from Kent shouting: "Ramsay Out, Bramleys in!" Then they sat outside my restaurant, covered in manure, eating sandwiches,' said Gordon.

So what finally ended the impasse, halted the legal action and caused Britain's toughest, angriest chef to apologise? Once again, it was his mother who forced him to do the decent thing. 'I did feel a bit guilty about the plonker reference because Mum said, "Gordon, you shouldn't talk about people like that when they are being nice to you." I don't give a toss about the farmers but I do care what my mother thinks,' he said.

It was the ultimate proof that the foul-mouthed monster in the kitchen was a very different man elsewhere. 'I put on a different coat when I go to work, like everyone else does,' he said. 'Yes, I get angry, yes, I swear and, yes, some people hate it. But I'm doing it for a specific reason, to get the very best results and create the very best food. I'm a different man inside and outside of the kitchen and I will never apologise for that.'

Nor would he apologise to those who inadvertently strayed into his kitchens – however important they were. While Gordon was earning some extra money running a massive outside-catering day at Royal Ascot that year, a man he didn't recognise came into the vast temporary kitchen looking for a cup of coffee. 'I stopped him, grabbed him and said, "What the fuck do you think you are doing in here? Get the fuck out and get your fucking cup of coffee somewhere else," and he scarpered.' The man turned out to be the managing director of the entire Ascot operation and was effectively paying Gordon's wages. He never got his coffee.

SEVEN

WHERE'S DAD?

It was Millennium Eve and Gordon was, of course, working. Extra chairs and tables were being squeezed into the main room at Gordon Ramsay, where he was hosting a massive party for more than a hundred family members and friends from around the country. As it was a private affair, Gordon had let any of his staff who didn't want the overtime to have the night off. And this had turned out to be just about all of them. So, as the world got ready to party, Gordon was in his kitchen, on his own, with a massive and important task ahead.

'Dad had died almost exactly a year before and my mother had wanted everyone together that night, so I wanted it to be a perfect evening,' Gordon said. He had gone to Chelsea at 8am to start the preparation work, pretty much like any other working day. But things didn't stay ordinary for long.

'I was working on the canapes, roast beef, the home-made pizzas for the children who were coming and everything else when I got a call from home. Tana hadn't been feeling well first thing and I had desperately wanted to stay at home and be with her. But I'd needed to come in because I was obsessed with getting everything right for the party and now she was feeling worse.'

Not sure what to do, Gordon suggested that Tana rest before the big night and told her to call him if she didn't feel better later. But, as it turned out, he called her first. 'A little bit later on, I rang to see if she could pick up some of the family from Euston station,' he says. Tana, so often criticised for putting up with her husband's chauvinism and insensitivity, had reached breaking point, however. 'She told me to fuck off,' Gordon remembers.

It turned out she had good reason. Tana was carrying twins and, while their due date was nearly five weeks away, it looked as if they were in a hurry to be born. Instead of being children of the new millennium, the new Ramsays were ready to be among the last to be born in the old. Their dad, however, was in complete denial.

'There were no staff working and I was up to my eyeballs in it, really up against it, when the phone rings. It's Tana, saying, "I've got tummy pains – I think it's contractions." So I said, "You're having a laugh, aren't you? Take some Nurofen and call me back in a couple of hours." I just went back to work yet again and tried to push it to the back of my mind.'

Tana, meanwhile, headed for the hospital. She called Gordon as she left but once again he failed to grasp the seriousness of the situation. Over the moon about how the preparations for the party had gone and how good the restaurant and the food looked, he was just upset that his wife might miss the fun. 'I told her to come straight to the party after the check-up,' he says, still convinced at that time that she would be given the all-clear. She wasn't. 'Two hours later Tana rings back and says, "They're taking me down now" and I said, "Down where?" and she says, "Into theatre." A doctor then came on the line and told me they were doing an emergency Caesarean in 15 minutes.'

At last, Gordon got the message and did what most soon-to-be fathers do in this kind of situation. He panicked. The family and other guests had started to arrive at the restaurant but he ignored everyone and went out into the street to grab a taxi. But it was the most important New Year's Eve in a thousand years and he couldn't find one.

'In the end, I started running, just running blindly through the streets like a madman.' Desperate by now, he was heading north towards the Portman Hospital, where Tana had long since been booked in to give birth. The hospital is a celebrity favourite, where women like Victoria Beckham, Zoë Ball and Sarah Ferguson had had their babies. But it is nearly four miles from the Gordon Ramsay restaurant and even when Gordon did finally flag down an empty taxi he got caught in traffic and it took what felt like for ever to get there.

By the time he finally arrived, Tana had two little surprises for him: a boy and a girl, soon to be named Jack and Holly. 'When I first saw them I couldn't believe how tiny they were,' he says, just like almost every other new dad. 'But they are so perfect.' In typical fashion, Gordon didn't stick around to admire the two new Ramsays for long, however. After a few tears with Tana and some hugs for the doctors and nursing staff, he was in a taxi, back to the restaurant and back to work.

Having already heard Tana's news by mobile, the family turned the party into a massive and well-oiled celebration. 'I got there at 1.10am and people were pissed as newts. All the family were blotto. I think I must have been the only chef in Britain who didn't have a drink that night,' says Gordon, even though he had more to celebrate than most. And for Gordon work still took priority over almost everything else in his life.

After the last guests had left, Gordon spent several hours on his own in Chelsea, cleaning his beloved kitchen. And even then he didn't go straight back to the hospital to see his wife and new children. 'It was about 7.30 when I left the restaurant. I went to a greasy spoon in Victoria and had the best cooked breakfast ever for £4.99. I was sitting there alone, it was New Year's Day, I'd had my first son and I'm thinking, Here I am, the happiest man in Britain today, having an English breakfast, and there are all these people looking at me thinking I was some sort of Nobby-no-mates and saying, "Look at that sad bastard on his own."'

Gordon's surreal calmness was soon shattered, however.

Back at the Portman, doctors had noticed a heart murmur in the baby boy and, with his birth weight just four pounds five ounces, they wanted him under constant observation to check it wasn't going to turn into anything more serious. Tana and the twins were kept at the hospital for two long, painful weeks while everyone's condition was monitored. 'When they first spotted it, they said it would be touch and go for the next 24 hours,' says Gordon, who then did stick to his wife's side as the first set of vital tests were carried out.

But soon little Jack was given the all-clear, and Gordon took Megan in to see her mum and her new brother and sister. He then found himself crying suddenly about how perfect his family life had become. He had built the life he had always wanted, both at work and at home. And he vowed to rewrite the history books and become the father he had never had himself – though this new policy may not have been immediately obvious to anyone else.

'It was very hard to visit the hospital because the restaurant was open, but Tana and I stayed in touch on the telephone. She is amazingly understanding,' he said, with amazing understatement, when describing the first two weeks of 2000 when Tana and the twins were still in the Portman.

In Gordon's defence, January is a big month for restaurateurs at his level. The books have to be balanced during the New Year lull, which tends to see takings fall after the seasonal excesses. And the publication of the latest Michelin ratings will reveal how well – or badly – you have done over the previous 12 months. As Gordon continues to say, being awarded Michelin stars is only the first half of the battle. Retaining them is equally important and can be even harder to achieve.

In January 2000, Gordon had another restaurant in the frame for official recognition. The previous year he and his old friend and protege Marcus Wareing had decided to put the traumas of Aubergine and L'Oranger behind them and open a new restaurant of their own. Their joint workloads were to move up a gear once more. The pair looked around all the high-rolling parts of central London and, ironically, the site that showed most promise was 33 St James's Street – just around the corner from the Ritz and less than a hundred yards from the 'under new management' L'Oranger.

After putting in a bid and winning, Gordon and Marcus got ready to open up. Gordon was to be the driving force behind the venture and his money and his reputation would be on the line if it failed. But as head chef Marcus would be the man in the kitchen every day making sure everyone lived up to Gordon's expectations. Petrus, named after Marcus's favourite wines, just as Aubergine had been named after Gordon's favourite colour, had just 50 covers and one of the most expensive wine lists in London. There were more than 300 choices on the wine list, including up to 30 Chateau Petrus bins.

As with anything to do with Gordon, the restaurant was to be judged primarily on the quality of its food, however. And shortly after Gordon's twins were brought home from hospital that January, he found out how well this judging had gone. Petrus had earned a Michelin star within just seven months of opening. The Ramsay magic was as potent as ever – and even more official recognition was just around the corner.

Later in the year, Gordon was up against Raymond Blanc and his old mentor Marco Pierre White in contention for Chef of the Year in the 'Cateys'. Gordon won the prestigious award, with the head judge saying, 'Ramsay's food is vibrant, the flavour of the moment, and is executed to the very highest level,' before adding the blindingly obvious statement that 'Gordon Ramsay can no longer be ignored'.

Meanwhile, Gordon Ramsay was named Top Restaurant of the Year in the latest internationally famous Zagat survey, and was shortly to be named Best Fine Dining Restaurant in the next *Harden's London Restaurants*. In recent months, two further Gordon Ramsay books, *A Passion for Seafood* and *A Chef for All Seasons*, had also joined the best-sellers. And, with *Beyond Boiling Point* getting an airing on television as well, it seemed Gordon could do no wrong or get no happier.

He was even able to laugh (after a while) when a rival restaurateur strode into Petrus one night, had a brief slanging match with the staff on the front desk and then spat on the wall before leaving – triggering a £1,300 repair job to the hand-woven wallpaper.

From the outside, it looked as if everything in Gordon's life was finally working out just perfectly. His restaurants were booming, his reputation was getting ever stronger. He was married with children and, despite working some of the longest hours in the industry, he was managing to be the father he had never had. His mother was more relaxed than she had ever been and his sisters were thriving.

Gordon was happy too. Catering really could be a contact sport and its challenges seemed as exciting as any of the ones he had hoped to face as a footballer at Ibrox. And in many ways the possibilities and opportunities available to him in his new world seemed even broader. He had already achieved a huge amount – but he still had enormous dreams for the future.

The problem, though, was that, for all the good news,

there was a secret cloud on the horizon, a worry that nagged away at him most days and almost every evening. And in the small hours of the night, when the restaurants and the kitchens were closed and his wife and three children were asleep, Gordon knew he had to face up to this private nightmare. He had to work out what to do about his brother.

EIGHT
THE FAMILY SECRET

Two boys, born less than two years apart. They shared a room, a love of fishing, a sense of humour and a passion for sport. Gordon reckons he grew up with a ready-made best friend in his younger brother, Ronald, and for years the boys were all but inseparable. 'We spent almost ten years sleeping in the same room together, me on the top bunk, him on the bottom always putting his feet under my mattress, pushing me to the floor,' says Gordon of the good times.

But the two best friends soon lost their way. By the time they were in their twenties Gordon had effectively lost Ronald to drugs and crime. In their thirties, the gap between the brothers was at its widest and most depressing point, as vividly illustrated by the events of Monday, 28 February 2000.

On that day, Gordon, as usual, was in the kitchen at

Gordon Ramsay, shouting, swearing, encouraging and demanding the best of his staff. He had a loving family, money in the bank and hopes for an amazing future still ahead. But on that same Monday a gaunt and pale Ronnie was waiting alone in a magistrates' court in Bridgwater, Somerset. He was there to be sentenced for stealing £70 worth of batteries from a supermarket to pay for his chronic heroin addiction. He had no partner, no income and no confidence in any aspect of his future.

The brothers, friends for so long, had pretty much seen a parting of the ways the previous year. Gordon still tried to speak to Ronnie on the phone almost every day – sometimes for up to 45 minutes at a time. But the last time they had seen each other face to face had been nearly six months earlier, when Gordon had taken a rare day off and arranged a day at Silverstone for them. Ronnie had just been though his most recent rehab programme and this time had seemed desperate to stay off drugs and turn his life around.

Gordon was jubilant at his brother's progress and was trying to keep Ronnie's mind focused on good things rather than dwell on the bad. The idea behind a day at the racetrack was to try to recreate some of the fun times of their childhood, to have a 'lad's day out', a bit of healthy competition, a few laughs, a chance to forget all their day-to-day cares. But it wasn't to be.

'The night before we were due to go to Silverstone, I went round to check on Ronnie and he was out of it. He'd been to King's Cross and used heroin. I was devastated. I wanted to scream at him but I knew it wouldn't do any good. In his adult life, Ronnie had been using drugs far longer than he'd been clean and it just devastates me to see such a young, talented life going to waste. Drugs for Ronnie are an escape. It puts his mind in a cloud and he doesn't have to deal with reality. He's never had a fixed address for more than six months, or a bill in his name. For Ronnie, life becomes easier the more oblivious he is. I feel like I've lost him and it just leaves me full of despair.'

The trip to Silverstone never happened and shortly afterwards Ronnie left London and went back to Bridgwater, near where their mother lived. From then on, Gordon began trying yet another way to get through to his brother, staying in almost constant touch by phone but keeping other contact to a minimum. It was the latest phase in what had felt like an endless, debilitating battle with Ronnie's addictions.

'What we are doing now is tough love. He has had to go out of my life and I haven't seen him since he relapsed because I am not going to allow my family to fall down beside him. It is all no good if I am just there funding his habit. I have given a hundred and ten per cent and now I have to close the door, shut down and live with it. I still love him as my brother but we're at the end of the road. It's his choice and I've done everything I can. Now it's down to him.' They were some of the saddest words Gordon had ever said.

At this latest low point, Gordon was facing up to the awful dilemma that comes to relatives and friends of all addicts. You are desperate to understand, to help and to support them. But you are terrified of what might happen when you do. 'You can't get close to them because if you do they will ask you for £10 for a hit,' Gordon said of the worst times. 'Now I just dread getting the phone call saying that he is dead.'

No one can accurately pinpoint why some people turn to drugs and others don't. No one can really say why some get addicted and others don't. For the Ramsay brothers the questions are even more baffling. As teenagers, both were tall, strong, blond, good-looking and funny. Friends say both had boundless energy for life and all its possibilities. Gordon had the football skills that took the family back to Glasgow. But Ronnie had pole position in their father's affections and as a teenager was happy to toss up his career options: the Army or an apprenticeship as a mechanic. Girlfriends, great mates, good times – they both had them all.

So when and why did it all go wrong? One theory is that it happened when the boys' parents finally split up after so many years of fights and unhappiness. Gordon says the break-up made him happy, as he felt his mother would finally be free to live the life she deserved. But Ronnie, he says, could have taken an alternative view. 'My brother is two years younger than I am and our parents' split affected him in a different way. Parents can put a huge amount of emotional baggage on their children and it can make or break them,' was one of Gordon's many attempts to understand the situation.

Whatever the triggers, Gordon says Ronnie began by smoking a little pot and graduated on to stronger drugs during a trip to Amsterdam with friends. Speed, ecstasy, cocaine and, ultimately, heroin followed. Gordon, his parents, sisters, the rest of their family and a host of mutual friends could only watch what was happening and try desperately to help. But nothing they ever did seemed to work.

As Ronnie's elder brother and childhood best friend, Gordon was the most involved in the younger man's life. Trying to save Ronnie had become a secret obsession – something into which Gordon poured huge amounts of his time and thousands of pounds of his money over the years. But much of the time it felt as if it was all wasted effort. 'It is the one thing I feel I have failed at,' he said in 2000, when Ronnie was due in court in Bridgwater. But still he kept on trying, however ugly, depressing and threatening the task became.

Over the years, looking after his brother took Gordon far from the professionalism of his business life and the glamour of his new show-business world. It took him into the secret, hidden underbelly of our big cities and small towns. And many times it made him physically sick with fear and depression. On one occasion, Gordon was persuaded to go with Ronnie to visit his dealers. Ronnie said that this was the one way he could break off his relationship with them, to see them in person and to tell them that he was getting clean, no longer using, no longer a customer to be fleeced and destroyed. But to do so he needed his brother's support.

'Ronnie said he wanted to stand in among the junkies to tell himself how strong he was. It was the biggest load of crap I have heard. He said, "I need to use it once more, to tell myself I don't need to do it any more." I felt like catching him by the scruff of the neck and giving him a good hiding.' But instead Gordon decided to give his brother the benefit of one more doubt, and see if his strategy could work. The memories of what he saw that day have horrified him ever since.

'The dealers have all got Rottweilers, three spy holes in their doors. They look like sacks of shit. The telly's on, they're wearing big white Puma trainers, not a speck on them. You've got to sit there: "How are you, mate?" when you just want to beat the crap out of them.' On another, equally doomed occasion, Gordon says his car was bricked as he waited outside a dealer's house while Ronnie tried to put another ultimatum to the people inside. 'These drug guys are seriously dangerous people and I think they thought I was the police,' he says.

Professional counselling and therapy would be equally shocking for both brothers. Gordon enrolled Ronnie on courses at a variety of clinics over the years. And, when Ronnie asked him to, Gordon would sit in on the sessions and try to offer whatever extra support he could. That was what happened when Gordon was working every hour of the day and night setting up Petrus and Ronnie had agreed to attend an eight-week detox and rehabilitation programme at the Priory in Roehampton, south-west London.

The Priory is famous as the place where troubled celebrities check in claiming to be suffering from dubious-sounding complaints like 'exhaustion' or 'stress'. It is, in fact, one of the most serious addiction-treatment centres in the country. The vast majority of its clients are not celebrities or famous names. Ordinary people from all walks of life go there, normally with anxious families like the Ramsays waiting nervously in the wings.

When you are at the Priory, you, and your family, are

treated like everyone else, forced to live by the same rules and regimes, to contribute to the same sessions and aim for the same results. So, however many business commitments he had, Gordon was expected to turn up for whichever sessions Ronnie needed him for. And, tough as they were, he didn't miss a single one. 'It used to reduce me to tears. I'd sit in the car for an hour afterwards, trying to come to terms with it. I couldn't bear seeing Ronnie that way. When you go to places like that, you realise you've got no problems in life. It makes me realise how lucky I am. The guys in there go to hell and back,' he said after sitting through one long series of emotional therapy sessions, desperately hoping that the message had got through to his brother.

And for a long while it seemed as if it had. When the £1,000-a-week rehabilitation courses were over Ronnie swore he was ready to stay clean and start afresh – and Gordon was convinced that they had finally turned the corner. Ronnie got a job in one of his brother's kitchens and, with some rare responsibility and structure in his days, he began to thrive. Gordon handed over some extra money each week so that Ronnie could take judo lessons, and everyone seemed happy and calm. So Gordon's voice cannot hide the anger when he admits that it all went wrong. Nor can he hide the fear that history will carry on repeating itself, and that his brother may be lost for ever.

'After all that security and support and going clean, he still goes out and relapses. He had the perfect opportunity to get better but when I found out he was using again I realised we had probably given him too much, too soon. I brought him into our house. He lived with Tana and me, we got him a job but it still turned into a total nightmare. He's done rehab three times. If I was asked to fund it again, I'd do it, but I know damn well it won't work. I've been let down so many times. He's stolen from me, he's been in Tana's bag. I've given him money for haircuts and the next minute he's on his mobile in the middle of King's Cross buying heroin.

'That's the scary thing. It's everywhere. To get him to stop, you'd have to put him on an island. It's grim, it's shitty, it's paranoid. I'm amazed by what his body has learned to tolerate. But if he's not careful he will kill himself. I don't know how long his immune system can hold out. It's a disgusting drug.'

And, as Ronnie continued to plumb new depths, so did Gordon. One particular occasion was most chilling of all. 'The deal was that he could have one more score, a £10 bag, before he went into rehab one more time. I had to sit and watch him use and it's tortured me ever since. He tied the arm, waited for the vein. Have you ever seen heroin? It's like mud, like rusty water that's been left in an old bath. I've been through some low points in my life but that was the shittiest thing I've ever witnessed. That was my brother, the man I grew up with, shared a room with. Now he is doing that. Hard to believe it's the same person.'

As if that wasn't enough, there were the times when a desperate Ronnie tried to persuade his brother to try drugs as well, believing it would help Gordon understand the pressures he was under and the battles he had to fight. Gordon, in tears, refused each and every time.

So could Ronnie ever recover, and could the brothers ever be reconciled? Suddenly, in the middle of 2000, hopes were higher than they had been at any time since, a year earlier, the fateful day at Silverstone had been arranged and then cancelled. After being spared a prison sentence for theft and placed on probation for two years, Ronnie spoke for the first time about the demons in his head.

'I am not proud of my addiction, I'm fed up with it – and that's coming from the heart,' he said. 'It began eight or nine years ago when my parents separated. It started off as an occasional thing when I was 24. Then my father died in January last year. I was his favourite son and that affected me. I fell back into drugs badly. My brother has been behind me all the way. He rings me every day without fail for 45 minutes at a time. My whole family are a huge support. So many times my brother has dropped everything, leaving his family and business behind to come all over the world to collect me when I am in trouble.'

Ronnie's solicitor, Nigel Yeo, also acknowledged the support Gordon and the rest of the Ramsay family continued to offer his client. 'Ronnie still receives a lot of support from his family and speaks to his brother daily. He has also been provided with a car by his brother to enable him to find work and to get to work. So he is anxious not to betray his family's trust. He has been free of drugs for one week, which is a start. He feels that if he is free of drugs for the next week he can get a job.'

Leaving court, Ronnie himself swore he could finally turn his life around. 'I feel quite positive now,' he said. 'I've got probation, which is what I had hoped for because I can get more help with counselling. I stopped my methadone prescription a week ago and I'm trying my hardest to keep clean this time.'

Some 160 miles from Bridgwater, Gordon kept his fingers crossed but knew he had to keep his distance. In their homes, his mother and sisters were doing the same. This time Ronnie might make it, they all hoped. This time he might be able to cross the line and come back to them all.

Gordon in particular was desperate to win back the best friend he had known as a child but rarely seen since. The rest of the year would be a vital test and, however hard Gordon worked in his kitchens, at his business or in his home life, Ronnie would always be at the back of his mind. 'Every time I look at a four-ring gas burner I imagine my little brother on the back ring, simmering away. You would have to be a very callous, hard bastard in life to conclude that you can write off any member of your own family.'

So maybe, Gordon thought, this would be the time that Ronnie would kick his habit and stay clean. Maybe Ronnie could once more be the brother and best friend he had been more than a decade earlier. Maybe this time Megan, Holly and Jack could have an uncle in their lives again. Maybe.

NINE

MICHELIN STARS

Like most men, at 18 Gordon had dreamed of owning a Porsche. But when he finally saved up enough money to buy his first car the reality was a little different. 'It was an old Fiat Strada that was fucking ghastly beyond belief. It was like going around in a baked-bean tin with a hairdryer for an engine, constantly farting.' His next car wasn't much better: a terminally uncool Austin Princess that he called 'the ugliest car in history'.

So the car Gordon collected in January 2001 is the perfect illustration of how far he had travelled in life. It was a blue Ferrari 550 Maranello worth a cool £152,000 and capable of up to 200mph. His wife Tana bought it, as a surprise, and handed him the keys on a very special occasion: the day he found out he had won a historic third Michelin star. Looking at his new car and holding the letter from Michelin left Gordon unsure about which excited him the most. 'I think from Monday to Friday the third star is the best news but from Saturday morning to Sunday it has got to be the Ferrari,' he finally concluded.

Nevertheless, the importance of the third star was hard to overlook. Awarded to Gordon Ramsay in Chelsea, it meant the restaurant was officially the very best in London. After a row with the Michelin organisation the previous year, Marco Pierre White and Nico Ladenis had both handed back their three stars. So in 2001 Gordon was safely at the top of his game and the very top of his profession. He was also busier than ever, with television producers knocking on his door almost as often as hungry diners. Having shocked Middle England with his language and his passion in the *Boiling Point* documentary, Gordon was preparing to do pretty much the same again in a controversial episode of the BBC's *Friends for Dinner* – before wooing all his critics back with an extraordinarily emotional episode of Channel 4's award-winning makeover show *Faking It*.

Picking Gordon to go on *Friends for Dinner* was seen as controversial because the show tended to attract the description 'cosy' in most television reviews. And that wasn't a word many people associated with Gordon Ramsay. The idea behind the show was simple. Ordinary people planning dinner parties would be filmed getting some extra tips from chefs or restaurant owners and could call them for advice right up until the event itself. It was all as far from the angry, hurly-burly world of a true professional kitchen as could be imagined. Or at least it was until Gordon agreed to take part.

He was matched up with 40-year-old management

consultant Simon Law and tension built up from the very start. 'Gordon who?' was Simon's reaction on being told who his mentor was going to be. And his interest in cooking didn't seem to improve much when he had been told. After inviting Simon round to Gordon Ramsay to watch the professionals at work, Gordon soon became convinced that the amateur chef wasn't really ready to learn – one of the greatest sins in the Ramsay book. 'I thought it would be a nice gesture to have him in my kitchen but it was two days of hell. He has not been told he is wrong in 30 years, he wasn't interested in learning and he was rude.' And this was while the two men were still getting along.

Things heated up one day when Simon rang his mentor for advice – at precisely the wrong time. 'It was 1.30pm and of course I was busy. The guy had the cheek to tell me not to panic and I said I wasn't panicking but I did have 49 people in the restaurant wanting lunch and they were more important to me than a management consultant who wants to be a star for the day. I threw the phone against the wall and then into the bin.'

It all made fantastic television, of course. As did the scene at the end of Simon's two-day spell in the Ramsay kitchen when the chef blew icing sugar over his protege in a moment of frustration – only to have the whole packet thrown over his head.

Having threatened to walk off the show altogether, Gordon pulled back from the brink, pretended he hadn't heard when his meringues were called 'naff' and even turned up as a guest at the obligatory dinner party Simon threw at the end of the show. 'Tense', rather than 'cosy', is probably the best word to describe that evening. 'He may be a vicious git in the kitchen but away from all that Gordon is actually a very nice guy,' was how Simon summed up the experience after the cameras has departed. Gordon, however, was even less prepared to mince his words than normal when asked about his would-be protege. 'The guy found it hard to understand discipline. He is a three-star Michelin plonker,' was his final verdict on his unlucky onscreen companion.

That certainly wasn't the kind of language Gordon would use to describe his next hopeful protege – a shy Geordie burger-van worker named Ed Devlin. As part of Channel 4's *Faking It* series, Gordon had been picked as one of the team who would try to convert Ed into a convincing head chef for an international haute cuisine contest in London. It was to be an inspiring, emotional, almost heartbreaking experience for all concerned.

The scruffy, unshaven, quietly spoken Ed certainly had a bad start on the show. The first meal he cooked for Mezzo chef David Laris and his wife was a disaster and then, with the cameras rolling, his duck in cranberry sauce came second to an eight-year-old girl's pan-fried salmon in a cooking competition for Brownies.

Fortunately, Ed was a fast learner and the quality of his food was soon judged to be up to standard. His problem was that he was useless at running a kitchen. He admitted he hated shouting at people, swearing or telling others what to do. And without that skill, Ed's mentors said, he could never fool the judges and fake it as a top chef. Which was where Gordon came in.

A week in Gordon's kitchen was seen as an essential way

for Ed to learn what a real chef looks, acts and sounds like. Ed was horrified from the moment he walked through the door. 'I thought I would never last the first day, let alone a week,' he said after less than two hours in the chef's company. 'I hate being rude or people being rude to me. I missed my home and when Gordon was shouting at me I felt like jacking it in because I just thought I didn't need all that.' And for a while it looked as if the pair would never get over their differences. 'I'm really glad I don't live in his head. It must be a really cold and sterile place. Having to be Gordon Ramsay for the rest of your life, that's like a curse,' was how Ed first viewed the man who seemed to have been yelling, 'I don't want to see a wimp – I can't stand wimps' at him from the moment they had met.

As so often happens with Gordon, it was a football match that ultimately brought the pair together. Gordon decided Ed should referee it, in order to learn more about authority, taking control and making decisions. It was a turning point for them both. 'I think it would have been very easy to leave with him thinking I was a dick and me thinking he was a twat,' Ed said later. 'And we could have carried on for the rest of our lives thinking that. But fortunately we reassessed our first evaluations.' A most unlikely friendship was born.

In the remaining days of the four-week shoot, Gordon worked harder and harder to toughen up his charge and get him ready for the competition. And when the time came Ed was up for the challenge. He led his team of chefs with Ramsayesque passion, created the three-course meal for 12 and won over all three of the expert judges in the haute cuisine competition. In the process he created what even American audiences voted one of the best-ever *Faking It* moments when the series was shown across the Atlantic the following year. Back in Britain, the reaction had been the same and the show had won Best Factual TV Moment in the 2001 BBC television awards.

What Ed was able to do after spending so much time with Gordon was give a rare insight into his character. He reckoned there was more to the man than the swearing and the stereotype – though he wasn't entirely sure what that was. 'Gordon is actually a very likeable guy and I won't have a bad word said against him. He is inspiring to be around and once he steps inside the kitchen he changes and comes alive. His enthusiasm is infectious and he has this fantastic ability to raise people above the merely exceptional to verging on the sublime. Outside of the kitchen, Gordon is quiet and shy. While I didn't get to know him very well, what I did know I liked. Mind you, I think you could spend 20 years with Gordon and still not know him any better.'

And, while the two men had struck up such an amazing rapport, it looked as if they would remain worlds apart when the show was over. Gordon invited Ed and his partner Martine to his London restaurant for a celebratory meal. But the couple stayed in the North-East. Ed, who left his old burger business and found a new job working full-time in the kitchens of Gateshead Council, was spending most of his time clearing tables and washing dishes. He harbours no ambitions for a career in show business or in a fancier kitchen. 'Gordon proves that to be a top chef you have to want it one hundred per cent, one hundred per cent of the time, and I don't. The show hasn't changed me at all. I think I am more appreciative of good food now and I know the effort and the science that goes into making an expensive meal. But I'm happy with my life and, while it is great that people still want to stop and talk about the show, I never wanted to be famous.'

Gordon, however, was fast becoming more famous by the year. And he was finding out that fame and fortune can both come at a price. What happened to his £152,000 Ferrari was a case in point. Within weeks of getting the car's keys, Gordon and his old friend Marcus Wareing had left Gordon Ramsay at the end of dinner service and headed down the Fulham Road for a 2am breakfast. While he was reversing into a parking space in front of the Vingt-Quatre restaurant, a woman in the queue outside stepped into Gordon's path. 'She slapped the back of my car for no apparent reason,' Gordon later told Marylebone Magistrates' Court, where the matter was finally resolved in his favour. 'I moved forward because she was shouting and banging her hands on the boot. I did not understand what was going on. I wanted to get out of the car but it was difficult because she would not let me out. I had to wind down the window and she was shouting: "Did you not see me? I was in the road." While the window was open, she was screaming at me in a high-pitched voice. She was saying that I was arrogant and boisterous. She said, "I don't like your arrogance, you arrogant chef." And she said, "What would you do if I scratched your car?"'

They were both shortly to find out. Gordon and Marcus headed into the restaurant for scrambled eggs on toast while trying to keep an eye on the lady from the street. 'When I went to pay the bill, I saw quite clearly through the window that she was leaning, slumped over the back of my car.' She had then come into the restaurant, tapped Gordon on the shoulder and laughingly apologised for scratching it. By this point, the police had been called, however, and in court the lady was finally told to explain herself and apologise. 'I just wanted to wind him up, play a trick, it was silly,' she admitted, before being found guilty of causing £1,500 of damage and fined £150 with £125 costs.

For his part, Gordon said the whole affair was made worse by the way his public persona had been dragged into court and potentially used against him. 'You have a reputation for losing your temper, don't you?' the defending counsel asked him at one point, presumably to suggest that Gordon had in some way goaded his attacker into action. And this was not the end of the Ferrari affair.

Less than three months later, Gordon and Tana, then pregnant with the couple's fourth child, were heading back into London in the car after a rare weekend break in Wales. At a roundabout in Hammersmith, west London, the driver of a Subaru decided to race them. He overtook the Ferrari before ploughing into the back of it and sending the Ramsays spinning into the central reservation. 'My whole life flashed before my eyes and I immediately thought of Tana,' said Gordon who immediately took his wife to the Chelsea and Westminster Hospital for a check-up. Tana and the couple's baby were fine, but what had turned out to be too high profile a car had been written off for good.

Away from the road, Gordon's amazing rise from a Glasgow housing estate to the very top of the culinary establishment looked set to pass a new milestone. There were rumours that the aggressive bad boy of British restaurants was to take over the kitchen at the oh-so-refined Claridge's in Mayfair. John Williams, the previous Maitre Chef des Cuisines there, was being moved sideways to look after the five-star hotel's other food offerings – and the owners wanted a new start for their flagship restaurant. But would they pick someone like Gordon? He would be 'a colourful choice for such a respectable hotel', one anonymous source told the *Evening Standard* when rumours about his possible appointment first surfaced.

But others said that over the years Claridge's had actually been proved a little more flexible to changing times than might have been expected. In 1945, for example, Winston Churchill had approved a plan to put a spadeful of Yugoslav soil under one of the beds in Suite 212 so that the room could be officially decreed Yugoslav territory when the exiled king's son was born there. Meanwhile, everyone from Margaret Thatcher and Nancy Reagan to Donatella Versace and the Beckhams held parties and booked rooms in the hotel. Perhaps Gordon Ramsay, in this company, might not raise as many eyebrows as expected.

And in the end Gordon did beat his rivals and win what had turned out to be the highest-profile and most hotly contested job in London's restaurant world. What was more of a surprise was the fact that he was allowed to put his name above the door. Gordon Ramsay at Claridge's opened in October 2001 after £2 million had been spent taking the restaurant's capacity down from 120 to just 65 and turning the room into a shrine to classic art deco style. Etched mirrors, elegant 1930s wall lights, woven-silk chandeliers and apricot-coloured silk wall coverings set the tone. Gordon's signature aubergine-coloured leather chairs stood around the circular tables and every piece of cutlery, china and glassware was chosen by Gordon himself.

Having timed the drive from his Chelsea restaurant to Claridge's at just seven and a half minutes, Gordon was ready to defy all his critics and control both kitchens simultaneously. 'Everyone is expecting me to fall, everyone is saying, "Oh, he's spreading himself too thin and Claridge's is going to be the death of him." But bollocks. The only people saying that are the jealous bastards who didn't work hard enough to be offered this kind of position in the first place,' he said, anger, spirit and confidence showing through in equal measure.

And Gordon did have some strong supporters. Claridge's general manager, Chris Cowdray, said he knew early on that the company had found the right man for his hotel's new venture. 'I get a buzz out of dealing with Gordon as he is so passionate about restaurants – and about this one in particular,' he said.

And in return a fired-up Gordon was entirely shameless about promoting it. 'A monster has arrived in London's posh Mayfair. It wasn't there two weeks ago, but it has roared in on a whirlwind of culinary interest and curiosity,' proclaimed the *Daily Mail* just after the big opening. But this was hardly independent comment: Gordon had written the article himself. 'Yes, it's my Gordon Ramsay at Claridge's restaurant,' he continued, coming clean in a feature of nearly 2,000 words. 'It is generating a hurricane of activity. Yesterday we received more than 500 telephone calls for reservations. And 300 faxes. The response has been phenomenal and, in only the second week, we have welcomed 1,500 clients. The breathing, sweaty monster lives in the telephone. Booking is open from 8am to 10pm – and there are four telephonists trying to secure the breach every time a fresh wave crashes through.'

A more naked promotional activity would be hard to imagine. But Gordon was determined to keep the tills ringing and ensure the money men behind Claridge's didn't ever regret putting their faith in him. And, fortunately, when it came to big money deals Gordon was fast gaining form.

A couple of months earlier, three City workers had come for dinner at his Petrus restaurant one Tuesday and spent an amazing £8,000 on Champagne. And that turned out to be just the beginning of an extraordinary week for the Ramsay finances. Two days later, six other quite unconnected City workers arrived at Petrus for dinner just before 9pm – and they didn't leave until they had spent a record-breaking £44,007.

Gordon says that when the men first arrived there was no sign of the spending that was to come. They had come from the City by taxi and two of them each ordered an ordinary £3.50 Kronenbourg beer while the others stuck with mineral water at the bar while they waited for their table to be cleared. Only when the group had finally taken their seats did the real drinking and spending begin. The first three bottles of wine they ordered were a Chateau Petrus Claret 1945, which cost a staggering £11,600, a 1946, which was a bargain in comparison at £9,400, and a 1947, which added another £12,300 to their bill. After their three-course a la carte meal and a few lesser bottles of wine, they decided they should have some dessert wine – and picked a 1900 Chateau d'Yquem at £9,200.

'They cleaned us out of our very best bottles – and they didn't bat an eyelid when they got the bill,' said Gordon, who had decided to knock the £400 the businessmen had spent on food off the total. 'They seemed to have enjoyed themselves tremendously and our wine waiter was absolutely ecstatic. For him it was just like winning an Oscar. It was an unprecedented evening.' As, indeed, was the four-figure tip the men left to be shared between the equally ecstatic waiting staff.

Back at Claridge's, things were not always going so smoothly, however. One afternoon, Gordon was striding through the hotel lobby towards the restaurant when an immaculately dressed older lady stood up and accosted him.

'Young man, I have waited to see you,' she began. 'Do you realise that I have been coming here for 42 years for lunch and now I am told that there isn't a table for me?'

'I'm sorry to hear this. Did you try to book?' Gordon asked nervously.

'I have never had to book before and I don't intend to do so now. What is more, I think it is appalling that the restaurant is so full. What happened to the days when one might take a quiet lunch with a friend without all this palaver?'

What indeed? For the Ramsay palaver wasn't just centred on Claridge's. In an emotional homecoming, Gordon was opening an equally sought-after new 70-seater restaurant in his old city of Glasgow. Amaryllis was to be his first venture outside London and ended a two-year quest to find a suitable Scottish site. It also helped him bury some demons. Since walking out of Jock Wallace's office nearly 15 years earlier, he had seen Glasgow as the scene of his biggest professional failure. So it meant a huge amount to him that he could finally come back there in triumph.

Amaryllis was opened as part of a massive refit of the super-stylish One Devonshire Gardens Hotel – in a city Gordon could hardly recognise from his childhood or his footballing days. Stylish shopping arcades, designer stores, boutique hotels – what had been 1990's European City of Culture had since discovered a new financial and social heart. There was big money there again and a Ramsay restaurant was just the kind of place people wanted to spend it. But were the locals really ready for menus promising 'veloute of haricots blancs with roasted ceps and grated truffle', 'tortellini of lobster and langoustines with fennel puree and baby spinach', 'cannon of new season spring lamb with caramelised shallots, caviar aubergine and basil and rosemary jus'? It seemed, right from the start, that they were.

The restaurant was praised as offering 'food of a standard as yet unavailable anywhere else in Scotland', according to *The Scotsman*'s food critic, Gillian Glover, who was one of the first people to try it. Other experts agreed, diners poured through the doors and within a year Amaryllis had been awarded its first Michelin star – one of the very few ever given north of the border. But, as with any Gordon Ramsay venture, there was controversy as well.

First of all, he had to deal with the pickets from Clydesdale Animal Action and Advocates for Animals who were demonstrating outside One Devonshire Gardens and demanding that foie gras be taken off the menu at Amaryllis. Gordon refused, claiming with difficulty that the geese were not being force-fed or ill-treated by his fair-play supplier. Next under the spotlight came the new restaurant's general manager. Gordon had picked old friend Fiona Nairn for the job, triggering a rash of speculation in the gossip columns. 'She is caring, welcoming, attentive, friendly – the perfect Scottish rose,' said Gordon of his new front-of-house manager.

But, more importantly to the gossips, Fiona was also the ex-wife of Scottish TV chef Nick Nairn, with whom Gordon had enjoyed a long-running feud – and whose own restaurant was just 15 minutes' walk down the road. 'I ate in Nick's restaurant and the only memorable thing was the awful shag-pile carpets,' had been Gordon's typically forthright verdict on his rival's former restaurant.

He had also heavily criticised his fellow Scot for spending too much time focusing on his television career rather than on his cooking. And, while this criticism would soon be levelled straight back at Gordon, it wouldn't stop him from speaking out. For, as his empire grew, the most opinionated chef in the country was about to unleash a series of extraordinary attacks on his rivals, his critics and his former mentors. Never one to choose an easy life or a low profile, Gordon Ramsay was going to hit the headlines like never before.

TEN

ON THE OFFENSIVE

It all began when Jamie Oliver started snapping at Gordon's heels. The irreverent Essex-boy chef had been a massive hit as far back as 1999, when *The Naked Chef* was first shown on television and spawned a series of best-selling cookbooks and other ventures. The youngster had fast become one of the most visible, and richest, chefs in the business, overshadowing many of his more experienced rivals. In 2001, the experts compiling the next *New Chambers Biographical Dictionary* added Jamie's name to their list, alongside Nigella Lawson and Rick Stein. Gordon Ramsay's name didn't make the cut, and it hurt.

Equally annoying, as far as Gordon was concerned, was the overconfident newspaper interview that 26-year-old Jamie had given the same year. 'I am the ambassador of British cooking across the world,' Jamie told the *Daily Mail*. 'I am the first cookery programme ever to be sold to

France, Italy and Spain. I'm in 34 different countries on 60 channels. I do all the big-name chat shows in America. I've done more for English food throughout the world in the past two years than anyone else had done in the past 100.'

Gordon thought differently – and in the first of what would prove to be a series of barbed comments he proved he would speak his mind whatever the consequences. 'My homage for contribution to British food goes to the Roux brothers,' he said in response to Jamie Oliver's claims. 'When they opened Le Gavroche in 1966, they changed the future of British cooking. What Jamie has done is to take away the intimidation of cooking. But there is a premier league – the serious chefs who cook serious food for a fully booked dining room every night. And then there are the TV chefs – and we all know which is which. Jamie is a talented guy, but he's got a lot to learn.'

Full-time TV chefs or celebrity chefs were to become a particular irritant to Gordon over the years – not least because he saw himself first and foremost as a restaurateur. 'These people are jumping all over the country on television but they haven't learned their craft,' he claimed. As part of that particular rant, he was happy to lay into shows such as *Can't Cook, Won't Cook* (which he always referred to as *Can't Wank, Won't Wank*). And he was equally happy to lay into their hosts. Ainsley Harriott of *Ready Steady Cook* was first in line for a Ramsay tongue-lashing. The show should be called *Ready Steady Twat*, Gordon declared, saying he thought Ainsley's real ambition was not to be a top chef but to present *Stars in their Eyes*. 'He's not a chef, he's a fucking comedian,' he said.

Meanwhile, he famously described his former Stratford-upon-Avon neighbour Antony Worrall Thompson as 'a squashed Bee Gee' and after Thompson appeared on *I'm A Celebrity ... Get Me Out Of Here!* he said, 'The man has more chips on his shoulder than McDonald's does in its freezer. He slags off every talented young chef. His biggest hang-up is he hasn't won a Michelin star. I don't need to go on television or down to the jungle with a thong on my arse to fill a dining room.'

Almost every other major name in British cooking also came under fire at one point or another. Gordon questioned the method used by Gary Rhodes to produce chips in his kitchen, while other top chefs were lambasted for hypocrisy. 'After *Boiling Point* was broadcast, loads of other chefs turned into hysterical bastards, jumping on the bandwagon to criticise me,' he claimed. 'Raymond Blanc went, "Oh, la la! We don't need this violence in the kitchen." Bullshit. When he flips his lid, he's like a Rottweiler.' He was also, according to Gordon, 'a little French twat' at times.

Not everyone was attacked directly when Gordon was in a bad mood, however. Some of his rivals appeared to be offered some praise – though there was always a sting in the tail. Nigella Lawson, for example, was effectively dismissed as decorative and a hindrance to real, professional cooking. 'She's sex on legs,' he said. 'Every chef in the country would love her in the kitchen, but we'd never get any work done.'

A long-simmering row also continued to flare up between Gordon and Sir Terence Conran, the founder of Habitat, who was widely seen as having transformed the nation's eating-out habits with the launch of carefully designed mega-restaurants such as Quaglino's and the perennially popular Le Pont de la Tour. At one point, Gordon said he would rather eat at his four-year-old daughter's prep school than at one of Conran's restaurants. Conran retorted that Ramsay's food was only fit for babies in the first place.

'I will stick to cooking and he should stick to designing ashtrays,' was Gordon's final, winning word as the two sides declared an uneasy truce.

Even Gordon's former mentor and most respected colleague Marco Pierre White took some blows in a long-running feud which blew hot and cold with the seasons. In the good times, Marco called Gordon 'an exceptional young man' and Gordon returned the compliment: 'I owe Marco a great debt. It was he who put me on the road to where I am today.' In the bad times, however, Gordon took a more sinister view: 'Marco now, as opposed to being Britain's best chef, is Britain's number-one manipulator. His manipulation has become better than his cooking. When you listen to Marco's philosophy, you've got to question: is it in the interests of him or the interests of you?'

Other former friends also saw Gordon turn on them – even the professional critics who could damage him if they ever decided to take revenge. One famous example was Fay Maschler of the *Evening Standard*. She says, 'I put Gordon on the map at Aubergine and we were quite good pals until I wrote a piece saying he was brilliant but that he frothed all his sauces. He did a kidney dish, which I described as looking like toxic scum on a stagnant pond. He told the *Independent* newspaper that I didn't know anything and asked why the *Standard* still used a photograph of me aged 21 when I was so old. I took exception to him saying I didn't know anything and as for the picture it helps preserve my anonymity.'

Other critics found they weren't being insulted by Gordon – they were being manipulated. In a rare compliment, Gordon said that the newspaper column of director turned ferocious restaurant critic Michael Winner was his favourite reading of the week. And the chef claimed he knew just how to keep on the man's right side and avoid a negative review. 'He is witty and a true foodie. The way to look after Winner is to never keep him waiting. When he has time on his hands, he will sit and criticise. When you remove one dish, you have to replace it with another immediately so he doesn't have a chance to put his head up and slag off the glasswork or the pictures.'

Dealing with Winner also means agreeing to his requests, however difficult, as another of Gordon's favourite anecdotes illustrates. 'He came in a couple of months ago and said to our maitre d', Jean-Claude, "I'd like that table over there." And Jean-Claude said, "Oh, la la, Monsieur Winner, that table is booked and it is for six and there's just two of you." He said, "Jean-Claude. I. Want. That. Fucking. Table." So Jean-Claude came running up to me in the middle of service and said, "Oh, la la, Monsieur Winner is being difficult." I said, "What's fucking new?" We explained that the table was booked for six people and Michael said, "Well, put them in the bloody bar, serve them Dom Perignon and tell them they are here as my guests. I. Want. That. Table." So he did it. And were the customers happy? Over the moon. Six free dinners. He is the most generous 60-something man in Britain.'

To his credit, being accommodated like this doesn't ensure Winner will automatically give people like Gordon good reviews, however. The critic must have had too much time to think about things when he next ate at Claridge's, as he wrote off the new Gordon Ramsay restaurant as 'considerably worse than what was there before'.

At the very top of the culinary establishment, not even the legendary Egon Ronay was safe from Gordon's sarcasm. When the 89-year-old doyen of restaurant guides brought out his first book in seven years in 2005, he gave a great mention to the flagship Michelin-starred Gordon Ramsay in Chelsea – something most chefs would have celebrated. But Gordon could hardly have been less impressed. 'I'm not particularly bothered about being in the guide. I mean, who exactly is Egon Ronay and what does he know about haute cuisine? Doesn't he usually write about pubs and motorway service station food?' was his instant putdown to reporters.

Speaking his mind like this seemed ingrained in the Scotsman's DNA. Keeping quiet to keep the peace seemed impossible for him. If he thought it, he said it. And to hell with the consequences. 'I suppose I am too honest. But I don't have to take rubbish from anybody and I don't have to lick anyone's backside just for the sake of it,' he said, as a way of defending himself. In theory, this should have made Gordon a whole army of enemies – and he was once ranked alongside Chris Evans and Mohamed Al Fayed as one of the worst people to work for in an ITV show called *Britain's Unbearable Bosses*. In reality, Gordon enjoyed a fantastic relationship with his staff, and he was keen to thank them as often as possible.

'I know that after the TV documentary *Boiling Point* people saw me as a foul-mouthed chef who was rude and arrogant with his staff. But without their loyalty and understanding I would never have been so successful. The real secret of success is the right people, without whom I would not be where I am today,' he said after collecting his first Chef of the Year 'Catey', for example. And behind the scenes Gordon proved to be a sensitive as well as an inspiring boss. He happily offered a job to a young chef who showed promise but was able to work only one day a week because of his heart condition. He also set up a scholarship for aspiring chefs where the winner gets £5,000 and a series of apprenticeships in his and other restaurants – with the possibility of a full-time job at the end. Running the scheme, let alone looking after the winner, takes time, effort and money. But Gordon reckons it is one way for him to repay his debts to the industry that took a chance on him when he was starting out.

'This is a great job to be in when you are in the premier division, but underneath it sucks, it's the pits,' he said when he was asked why he had launched the scheme. 'It's a pressured lifestyle but even when you earn just £100 a week you have to be on your edge and dream of playing alongside the best. It's really tough for chefs trying to set up in business today.'

The chefs who do end up working with Gordon tend to stay with him, however. Some 75 per cent of the staff who had been employed alongside him in Aubergine in the mid-1990s were still working with him in one restaurant or another a decade later. Many were in top jobs, building up top reputations and winning Michelin stars under the

Ramsay umbrella but in their own names. Marcus Wareing at Petrus, Mark Sargeant at Gordon Ramsay at Claridge's and David Dempsey at Amaryllis are just a few examples.

Yorkshire-born Jason Atherton was to be next in line. Gordon was making Jason head chef at Verre, the new restaurant he was opening at the Dubai Creek Hilton Hotel in the United Arab Emirates. And the chef said the real Gordon Ramsay was very different from the public perception of him. 'He's certainly not a nightmare to work for. In fact, he's brilliant because he's straight-talking and he helps you move up the ladder. Too many other chefs are threatened by talented, younger staff, but if Gordon sees a talented chef he takes them under his wing and then, when they are ready to fly, gives them their own restaurant.'

'I want to have the Manchester United of kitchens and I love watching chefs who I have taught go on to be independent young businesswomen and businessmen,' said Gordon of his various proteges. 'Some of the big chefs don't seem to nurse the talent in their own kitchens. They just want to roll out branded chain restaurants that could be staffed by just about anybody. But I don't want to do that. I want to roll out the talent instead. The way I see it, if the people I've taught don't go on to be big stars in their own right I've fucked up. People think I struggle for staff because I'm an arsehole to work for. But I guarantee my staff complete honesty which is important when you spend so many hours a day together. I know my guys put their lives on hold for me, so I want it to be worth their while.'

As part of this policy, Gordon tries to ensure staff can do

a full week's worth of hours over four shifts, not five, so they can get 'one full day to sleep, then two days for a proper break'. Tips are shared between kitchen as well as waiting staff and even the insults are handled well. 'He knows how to bollock you and still be your mate,' was how footballer Tim Cahill described former Millwall boss Dennis Wise. Exactly the same was said of ex-footballer Gordon Ramsay.

Of course, that didn't mean that life was always easy in a Gordon Ramsay kitchen. While trying to be fair and inspiring, Gordon made no bones about being a fantastically demanding boss with a tough-love approach to teaching. 'The waiters know that I charge them for breakages, for example,' he said of his company-wide policies. 'I pay for the first breakage, but after that they have to pay and it is surprising how long it takes to break that second plate. I pay for perfection, not accidents and mistakes.' Step further out of line than just breaking a plate and even worse can be in store for you. 'There was a cook once who came in to work in my kitchens in London and stole my recipe book,' he said. 'I gave him a chance and asked if he was stealing and he said no. Well, I searched his bag and there it was – my recipe book. So we stripped him, wrapped him head to toe in cling film and left him outside the front door. He certainly didn't steal again for a long time, that's for sure.'

Anyone horrified about the way Gordon treated the people he worked with or competed against were also in for a shock in 2001. He was about to broaden his verbal broadsides to lay into a whole host of new targets. Just because Gordon didn't know you personally didn't mean he wasn't ready to insult you. As traffic wardens, taxi drivers, women drivers and, in fact, women in general were all about to find out.

Traffic wardens were the first to feel the Ramsay wrath. Calling them 'cockroaches', he reckoned he paid them up to £1,000 a week in fines – but never got as much as an acknowledgement in return. 'I have never met a pleasant traffic warden. I have never met a smiling one, a happy one, someone who actually says "Good Morning" to you. They are all just standing there, lurking in the bushes waiting to give you a ticket. And the better the car, the more they like ticketing it. The worst thing about the congestion charge in London is that the fucking cockroaches are infesting the streets even more than they did before it was introduced. They creep out of the concrete sometimes. I even check the boot to see if there is one skulking inside. If I'm three minutes over time for a meter out jumps a fucking cockroach. I'd rather work for the Vegan Society than be a traffic warden.' And all this is said with him hardly drawing a breath.

Next in line for a roasting were London taxi drivers, who he said drove him up the wall with their unwanted opinions, high prices and work-to-rule attitudes – though he soon regretted that outburst when he found out that none of them would pick him up on the street any more. 'I didn't win any mates with that,' he admitted afterwards. 'Now I'm running a marathon to raise money for the cab drivers' children's charity to apologise.'

And still the random criticisms came. When Chelsea and England footballer Frank Lampard was photographed shirtless with his chest and armpits shaved, Gordon was right in there with an opinion. 'Lampard looked absolutely ridiculous. You could never have got anything like that when I was playing football. The England team should be thinking more about football and less about their appearance, considering how they did at Euro 2004. Footballers are turning into women.'

Ah, women. Over the years, Gordon Ramsay's various musings on women have become legendary and it all began when he decided to speak out about women drivers. 'They frustrate the hell out of me and there's only one way to cut down on traffic congestion,' he told Paul Merton on BBC TV's *Room 101*. 'Give women drivers alternate days on the road. Have you seen them trying to get into a small space? They're stressed. They're flustered. They're on the mobile talking while taking seven or eight goes just to get into the space. Maybe if they could just drive on a Sunday and leave the roads to us from Monday to Saturday it would be a lot easier.'

Female workers were next in line for some shocks. If women work in a kitchen you can never get to use the toilet because they will always be in there crying, sorting out their make-up, gossiping with each other or resting from PMT, Gordon once said. Women at work also took time off because of 'morning sickness and women's troubles' and ruined all the banter with male staff in the kitchen. 'Men talk about totty all the time in my London restaurants but women don't enjoy that kind of talk,' he complained. Oh, and he said he could never have married a female chef because of her 'stinking of food all the time in bed' and claimed that the sight of women in the workplace might put him off sex. 'Just the thought of women sticking their hands up a pigeon's arse – it's not what would make your sex life fruitful,' was his considered opinion.

Professional women, not surprisingly, were outraged by what they heard. 'Ramsay is a brilliant chef but he makes me angry. It sounds like he is the one suffering from permanent pre-menstrual tension. A lot of women have been held back in the industry because of attitudes like Ramsay's,' said Lorraine Ferguson, one of the country's few female success stories, who had worked at the top restaurant L'Escargot in London.

'It sounds as though Ramsay is scared because there are wonderful women chefs and cooks around. To suggest that women are too emotional to work in his kitchen is pathetic,' added Lady Claire Macdonald, a former judge on television's *Masterchef*.

Finally, Sally Clarke, the legendary female chef whose Kensington restaurant Clarke's has been a foodie favourite for more than two decades, had a subtle dig of her own to make against Gordon and the other male super-chefs. 'Of course there are women in the industry. It is just that they are not clowning about as celebrity chefs on television or staring out of the pages of the colour supplements, so you are less aware of them,' she said. The last point was particularly well aimed. Gordon hadn't just been staring out of the pages of Sunday supplements in any old photographs recently. He had just been posing naked save for a well-placed conger eel in yet another bid to drum up publicity for his books and his businesses. (He joked with the paper's reporter that only the conger eel had been big enough to preserve his modesty and he enjoyed hinting yet again about the real reason why he had been nicknamed 'the Horse' by his Rangers teammates as a teenager.)

Joking aside, Gordon was actually more of a mischief-maker than a misogynist. Making outrageous statements to reporters made him laugh, kept the press happy and got him through the day. And back in the kitchen he was, in fact, very female-friendly. One of his longest-standing colleagues, Angela Hartnett, was being groomed for great things – soon to follow Gordon's other proteges with a restaurant of her own. And Gordon said he was 'over the moon' when 20-year-old Gemma Blow – the only woman among the five finalists – was announced as the winner of the first Gordon Ramsay Scholarship in September 2001.

One subject Gordon was less able to joke about was the general standard of cooking in Britain. When it was done badly, or when the industry was brought into disrepute, he really could let rip. 'I've just read about a hotel in Scotland that has gone public announcing the fact that they are doing a deep-fried sandwich full of Nutella,' he told reporters, appalled. 'I mean, Christ! Seventy-five per cent of my staff are French. They look at me like I'm some kind of twat because my Scottish brothers are launching two slices of bread with a fucking inch of Nutella between them, battered and deep-fat fried. Now what the fuck is this country coming to? What are we doing to ourselves? That has to be abolished. Here we are, progressing tenfold, buying the right bread, real croissants, we're making fresh muesli and we understand what a great cup of coffee is. And then some idiot brings out a deep-fried chocolate sandwich.

'I want to find the bastard that put that idea together. I've got the most amazing charcoal grill in my new kitchen. I'm going to sit his butt on it and criss-cross my name on his bloody arse cheeks to remind him. Is he fucking stupid? When these things hit France, the French just have a field day laughing at us. So I'm looking for that scumbag. I'm going to brand him with a hot iron like a little calf or a lamb. I'm going to put "Ramsayfield" on his butt so every time he wakes up in the morning he thinks, Fuck, I shouldn't have done that. That man is my new target and I'll find him.'

ELEVEN

BACK TO WORK

'On a warm summer evening in a restaurant kitchen in Chelsea, London, there is something resembling a ballet going on. A strange surreal ballet of 15 blokes in striped aprons, chopping, stirring, arranging with meticulous care, moving with such precision, such orchestrated timing, that they are almost as one as they count down the crucial timing on a dish of lobster tail ravioli. Out in the front of house, where immaculate staff are discreetly attentive and the decor is muted, there is an air of anticipation among those who seek the ultimate dining experience; an uneasy sense that at any moment something dangerous and exciting could happen. For this is Gordon Ramsay's restaurant and the artiste is not a predictable man.'

Reporter Susan Chenery of *The Times* perfectly summed up the tensions that lay beneath every meal at one of

Gordon's restaurants. 'With every perfect, pricey plate comes a tale of human suffering,' she wrote. 'There is a frisson of fear in the foie gras and a sous-chef clamped in a half nelson etched into the passion fruit cornetto.'

By the spring of 2002, Gordon Ramsay was already as famous for his anger and his volatility as he was for the quality of his food. So, while his latest restaurant was an obvious choice when Cherie Blair was planning a party for her husband's 49th birthday, it was still making the Prime Minister's protection team a little nervous. One wrong word from someone at the table could start the insults or the food flying, they feared. And, to make matters worse, the table Cherie had chosen wasn't exactly a standard one. She had booked 'the chef's table' – set directly in the kitchen and only yards from where Gordon himself would be screaming out his orders, wielding the knives and directing the entire lunch service.

The idea behind a chef's table is to give diners a dramatic and totally unique dining experience and it had been a huge hit with customers since Gordon had introduced it at Claridge's the previous year. By the time the Blairs made their booking, it had already been used by Andrew Lloyd Webber, chat-show hosts Richard Madeley and Judy Finnegan, Rolling Stone Ronnie Wood and models Jade Jagger and Kate Moss. Everyone had also paid heavily for their experiences: accounts showed that this one table alone generated around £1.2 million a year for Gordon's company coffers.

To reach the table, customers have to walk through the hotel's main art deco restaurant and follow the staff through the swing doors into the kitchen. There, backed on three sides by frosted-glass walls, is the slightly raised table surrounded by rich leather banquettes. As ringside seats go, you can't get any closer to the heat or the action and, while a dressed-down Tony Blair didn't take advantage of the opportunity, you can also have a full tour of the kitchens during your meal. No less than you might expect when your table's bill for lunch comes in at an average of £480 before drinks.

'Mr Blair stood up from time to time to get a better view of what was going on. He was particularly interested when a little fracas broke out between a couple of the sous-chefs,' one onlooker told the papers afterwards.

The Prime Minister also had a different shock a little later. Cherie had spotted Cilla Black in the main dining room and had asked her to burst through the kitchen doors to shout: 'Surprise, surprise!' halfway through the lunch. Ever the self-publicist, Gordon was happy to provide the Prime Minister's verdict on the experience when the four-hour celebration was over. 'He absolutely loved it. He was very relaxed and ate all the food we offered him. He was very interested in the way the food had been cooked and he seemed to enjoy watching all the chefs at work.' Even the Blairs' vegetarian security guard, it seemed, had been happy with the meat-free tray he had been presented with as he sat guarding the doors.

Back at home, the Ramsay family was still growing – not bad for a man who had said at the start of his marriage that he had a low sperm count because of spending so much time in front of hot ovens. At first, Gordon had an unorthodox name in mind for his third daughter. 'It sounds daft, but she looks like a Coriander. That's the name that came into my head as soon as I saw her.' But in the end he agreed with Tana that the name Matilda might raise fewer eyebrows in later life.

But what was both raising eyebrows and making headlines in the meantime was that once more Gordon had failed to be at his daughter's birth. Missing Megan's birth in 1998 could be put down to an oversight, the newspaper columnists and commentators seemed to feel. Missing Jack and Holly's birth on New Year's Eve 1999 could be seen as an accident. But missing Matilda's as well looked like a little more than just carelessness.

And, upfront as ever, Gordon was happy to confirm to everyone that a deliberate pattern had in fact emerged. He hadn't been at the latest birth because neither he nor Tana had wanted him there. And neither of them saw any reason to apologise for their decision.

'We have a very active sex life and we both contemplated over a bottle of wine that it wasn't good for our sexual relationship for me to be at the childbirth. I told her that I would feel squeamish seeing that level of mess. It's like sending 25 vegans into a kitchen with meat in the blender. So I was very relieved when Tana said, "I don't want you there. I won't feel attractive." I said, "Thank God for that." If Tana had turned around and said, "I want you there, it is an awful position and I need someone I deeply love by my side," then of course I would have been there. But that wasn't the case. She didn't want me to witness her distress. The truth is that I am a control freak. And in the delivery suite I wouldn't be in control, would I? I'd be standing there, useless, amid all the blood and the pushing and the sweating, like a useless prick.'

For her part, Tana says she knew her husband too well to expect him to cope properly with the reality of childbirth. 'I just wanted to get on with it and have Gordon there afterwards,' she said. 'I just wanted to have the babies clean and wrapped in a blanket and then be able to present them to him. He's squeamish enough when he cuts his finger after all.'

For all this, the couple continued to be roundly criticised for their unconventionality – and for their honesty. Gordon in particular came in for a lot of flak after going public about his views and his perceived chauvinism. But he remained defiant – even to his friends. 'There are dads I know who say, "I can't believe you missed the most momentous time of your marital life." I'm like: "Has your missus told you to say that? Is she wearing the trousers in your relationship?" Let me decide what I want to do at childbirth. The children's birthdays are phenomenal. The first time I took Jack fishing was phenomenal. But childbirth? It's like being stuck in a room with a thousand skinned rabbits.'

Or worse – because, when it came to labour, Gordon's imagination had clearly gone wild and he was prepared to come right out and say what most of his friends were too afraid to admit to thinking. 'I had images like something out of a sci-fi movie whenever I thought about childbirth – skinned rabbits and conger eels coming at me from everywhere. I didn't want that to be in my memory. Seeing a woman in distress, screaming at the top of her voice, pushing, pushing, pushing and sweat, sweat, sweat? I'd rather be stark bollock naked in a steam room with 50 vegans,' he said – his worst nightmares coming back around to food, as they always did.

With four children and a growing fortune, the Ramsays had long since moved out of their top-floor converted flat in grimy Stockwell. They now lived slightly further west, in a massive 11-bedroom home in the altogether leafier borough of Wandsworth. The new home had cost an impressive £3.5 million and the couple had spent an estimated £1 million refurbishing it and fitting it out before moving in. The biggest job was converting the building's four flats with an external staircase back into the glorious single-family home it would have been in Victorian times. And, when that was done, one of the Ramsays' first tasks had been to sort out the one design feature that would set them apart from almost every other house in Britain. For, while an increasing number of well-off couples now boast 'his and hers' bathrooms, the Ramsays can point to separate kitchens as well. Tana's was on the lower ground floor – Gordon described it as 'an MFI job' from where she could cook family meals and run the house. It was also where she frequently stocked up the family fridge with Jamie Oliver's ready meals from Sainsbury's – just to wind up her husband.

Gordon's kitchen was different. Nearly £500,000 different. His state-of-the-art room included a £67,000 main oven which was the size of a car and had to be lifted over the whole house and into the new kitchen by crane. Around it are cupboard-door handles based on Ferrari gear-sticks and costing £350 a piece, double dishwashers and a £480 silent extractor fan that Gordon said 'makes Megan's hair stand on end when we put her underneath it'. Then there is nearly £110,000 of limestone flooring, a sound system loaded with 2,000 hours of music, the best black Zimbabwean granite worktops money could buy – the list could go on and on.

What that list would also include, if Gordon had had his way, is a lock on the door. This mega-kitchen was to be his personal, private domain. No one else would be allowed to cook or mess about there. It would be where he works on new recipes and food combinations; where he indulges in his original love for food, without having to worry about customers on the other side of the wall or his children's dirty fingerprints and spillages. Because, having avoided being at the birth of all four of his kids, Gordon was determined to avoid a whole lot of their other inconveniences and irritations as well. 'I will never be a hands-on father,' he admitted unashamedly when asked about his home life and drawing a firm line between it and his professional world. 'I don't contact Tana when I can't get hold of scallops and I don't want to know if she runs out of Pampers.'

It was an interesting admission, because Gordon was also prepared to admit he only had the very sketchiest idea of what Pampers actually were. Triggering what seemed like an endless amount of criticism, he said he had never changed a nappy in his life – and didn't intend to start now. 'I hate the smell of poo,' he offered as a very simple justification. 'I can't go back to work and get excited about pesto if I've been smelling poo. I love all my children dearly, but wiping bums? That's not for me. I can put my hand on my heart and say I have never scraped pureed mango from a nappy. I can't get involved in that at all and I won't.'

Luckily for him, Tana was happy to accept her husband's

unfashionably unreconstructed male attitude. 'It has always surprised me how much it bothers other people that he has never changed a nappy,' she said as the children grew up. 'He is constantly criticised for it to this day but it never bothered me in the slightest. We have never had a situation where he has actually needed to do the changing. When the children were in nappies, Gordon was out working and I was at home being a mum and totally enjoying it. That was my job.'

In those early years, Gordon's view was that it was also Tana's job to get up in the night whenever any of their four children needed anything. 'If the babies cry in the night, my head is firmly stuck under the pillow. I have very little sleep anyway, so when I do sleep it has to be consistent. The babies have one bottle feed during the night. I can't come back from the restaurant and have to start looking around for powdered milk or Horlicks or whatever it is they put in there.' To his credit, Gordon was always entirely upfront about these uncompromising attitudes to raising his children – and he wasn't going to act a part in public which he didn't live up to in private. 'Tana once mentioned those bag things for carrying babies on your front and I said, "You've got no chance, sweetheart, if you think I'm walking through Battersea Park wearing one of those. Thanks, but no thanks."'

Nappies, sleepless nights and baby-slings apart, domestic life chez Ramsay continued to be happy. And work continued to be busy. After a lot of soul-searching Gordon had agreed to take part in another fly-on-the-wall television documentary in 2002 – some three years after *Boiling Point* had made him one of the most famous chefs in the country. This time the show, on BBC2, had a slightly different focus. *Trouble at the Top* was part of a series following business people facing big challenges. Gordon's latest professional challenge was to extend his restaurant empire into the dining rooms of yet another luxury hotel. And, as usual, he wanted all the publicity he could get.

The hotel in question was the grand old Connaught Hotel in the heart of Mayfair. Named after Queen Victoria's third son and described as 'a country manor in the heart of London', it was famous for its hushed, utterly discreet service and antique-filled public rooms. A Gordon Ramsay restaurant was going to be a massive wake-up call for its rich, aristocratic regulars. And it wasn't to be just any Gordon Ramsay restaurant – the man the *Daily Telegraph* called 'a hitherto unknown champion of women's rights' was putting his long-time protege and colleague Angela Hartnett in charge of the kitchen there. It was the latest in a long line of promotions for Gordon's loyal lieutenants and it made Angela the first female head chef at a British five-star hotel.

Gordon, however, remained as politically incorrect as ever when asked if this choice proved he had changed his mind about women chefs. 'If people think I have a pair of balls, they should wait until Angela gets going,' he told reporters as the new restaurant prepared to open. 'It's a real turn-on when she lets rip. You just close your eyes and think of her dressed up in boots and fucking cling film … nude.'

Angela, ignoring the latter description, was the first to admit that women chefs had to leave at least some of their femininity at the kitchen door. 'You have to become hard, you have to become tough,' she said. 'You learn to swear like a trooper with a thesaurus. I swear so much more than any other woman I know.'

It was Gordon who was to be swearing (under his breath and at himself, for a change) a little later, after the new restaurant at the Connaught had successfully opened. Angela was cooking up a storm there, the *Trouble at the Top* cameras had gone and the show had aired with decent audience figures and Gordon was looking forward to his 36th birthday. In typical fashion, he wasn't planning any major celebration, just a typical 18-hour shift at his flagship, Gordon Ramsay. But the night was to end very badly.

While Gordon was overseeing the final cleaning of the restaurant at nearly 3am, a customer who knew it was his birthday sent a bottle of Champagne into the kitchen as he left, saying the staff should share it and toast their boss's health. After doing so, Gordon helped lock up, got in his new Aston Martin and headed home. Two things then went awry. First, he took a wrong turn and started driving the wrong way down a one-way street. Then he realised that halfway down the street was a police station – outside of which two officers were standing having a cigarette and watching him carefully. 'They pulled me over, asked me whether I was aware I was driving the wrong way, then they breathalysed me and said I was over the limit. I was horrified, devastated. I had literally only had a glass of Champagne and I didn't even finish it.'

A procedural error meant Gordon escaped a drink-driving charge and a ban, however. Having taken him across town to London's West End Central Police Station in the early hours, they had failed to offer him the chance to take a urine or blood test – both of which are more accurate than a simple breath test. So the charges against him had to be dropped.

Gordon, saying he was 'absolutely mortified' and that he would 'never get in a car knowing I was over the limit', had been lucky. Unfortunately, his run of good luck was about to change. Just when so much in his life was going well, something terrible would bring him crashing back down to earth, as it always did. The man who had so nearly lost his younger brother to drugs was about to lose his closest friend in exactly the same way. The friend was fellow chef David Dempsey. And the way he died is something Gordon says he will never forget.

In many ways, David was a mirror image of both Gordon and his brother Ronnie. He too had been born amid some of the meanest streets of Glasgow. He too had had a distant, difficult father: his French-Mauritian dad had left the family home and moved to England when David was just five. And, like Gordon, David saw restaurant kitchens as an adrenalin-filled escape from everyday life, a place where he could take control, head up a team and create something truly special. Most of all like Gordon, David was fiercely ambitious and famously hard-working.

His work ethic had begun when he was working full-time at the New Maharajah restaurant in Glasgow's Sauchiehall Street. Like all major kitchen jobs, it was a tough, relentless and exhausting experience. But, instead of walking away on his days off, David agreed to work unpaid in a series of other city-centre restaurants and hotels in order to boost his CV and his experience. And after exaggerating the credentials on that CV – just as Gordon had done – David too got out of Glasgow. He blagged a job at Raymond Blanc's iconic Le Manoir aux Quat' Saisons restaurant in Oxfordshire, where his education really began and his life would change for ever. For it was on a rare night off from his job there as a chef de partie, or senior section head, that an exhausted David flicked on the television and saw the infamous *Boiling Point* documentary about Gordon Ramsay. Just as Gordon had made an instant decision that he had to work with Marco Pierre White back in 1986, so David made the instant decision to work with the wild, angry, passionate man he could see on his television screen.

He got the number for Aubergine and rang every day until he finally got to speak to Gordon himself. 'I've seen you on the television and I want to work with you,' he said, getting straight to the point in typically blunt fashion. Gordon had to laugh – almost everyone else was telling him they had seen him on television and wanted to lock him up in a mental hospital. Right from the start, he wondered if he could find a kindred spirit in the ambitious young Scot on the phone. So he offered him the chance to work a single shift at Aubergine to try to prove himself.

David's first task that early morning came when Gordon handed him a box of leftovers from the night before. 'I watch new chefs and, if they show those trimmings respect, as they would a main ingredient, then you can tell that they care about food and aren't just blase about only cooking foie gras or white truffles,' Gordon says. His next test for potential new chefs is even more prosaic. He likes to see them make a simple omelette, believing that you cannot go on to build far greater things unless you have the right foundations in place for the basics.

Within two hours of arriving at Aubergine that morning, David had passed his first two tests. When Gordon found out that the man was there on his first day off after working 14 consecutive shifts at Le Manoir, he passed his third. This kind of ambition, energy and dedication ticked every box on Gordon's mental recruitment sheet. 'I saw the potential in David, right from the start,' Gordon said, so he offered him a job as commis chef at Aubergine. It was one step down the ladder from Le Manoir but both men saw it as a potential springboard to better things. Both of them were right, and over the years their mutual professional respect and their friendship grew.

'The only thing we have ever disagreed on is football. He supports Rangers and I support Celtic,' David once said of his boss. Talking about women was another thing that brought the pair together. They would sit in the empty restaurant long after the final customers had left some nights, chewing the cud about relationships, life and love, winding down after the long, high-pressure shifts that inspired but exhausted them.

Elevated to the role of junior sous-chef at Gordon Ramsay by the start of 2001, David was to get a huge shock when Gordon sat him down at the end of one typically late night. 'How do you fancy heading back to Glasgow?' David was asked. Gordon was offering the 29-year-old the role of head chef at Amaryllis and David couldn't say yes fast enough. 'It was an opportunity I would probably never get again. Gordon has done more for me and my career than anybody else ever had or ever will,' he said of his mentor and friend.

A massive eating tour of Scotland followed, as the pair

checked out the competition before agreeing the style and the menu for Amaryllis. And David had high hopes for the future. 'It has been my ambition since I was young to achieve Michelin-star status and to be able to come back home and do it is obviously important to me. And once I've got my first star I will definitely want to push for a second.' Once again, the two men could hardly have been closer.

When both men were running restaurants, it became obvious that their temperaments, too, were similar – as one unhappy diner found to his cost when he questioned the food he was served at Amaryllis. Maurice Taylor, a restaurant and hotel owner of 40 years' standing, said his main course of pigeon was underdone. David, to put it mildly, did not agree. Maurice said he and his companions were then shouted at and effectively frog-marched out of the restaurant – in front of all the other diners. 'He came storming out of the kitchen asking what my problem was and coming on very strong. I am not used to being spoken to like that. And to have someone come out of the kitchen in his dirty whites to shout at us was unbelievable. Mr Dempsey could be a talented chef but his customer-relations skills are zero. It is very disappointing that he cannot handle hearing another point of view.'

'It seems as if Gordon Ramsay's fiery temper and intolerance of criticism has been passed on to his staff,' wrote the *Daily Mail* when it took up Maurice's story.

The diner agreed. 'Gordon Ramsay has done a great deal for the quality of food in Scotland and is a very talented and creative chef. But he has a reputation as a bully and it looks as if members of his staff are a reflection of their boss,' he concluded.

One set of people were prepared to put incidents like this out of their minds, however. The Michelin judges loved what they saw, heard and ate when they made their secret visits to the restaurant. David got his Michelin star less than a year after opening the restaurant doors. Gordon was equally ecstatic and was secretly planning even better things for the chef he described as 'like my little brother'.

When the hours at Claridge's were getting too long, Gordon was looking for a new £50,000-plus head chef to take some of the heat back at Gordon Ramsay in Chelsea. That man was to be David – and the old friends were glad to be able to spend more time together again. By this point, David had three children and Gordon had four. Both had large numbers of friends and colleagues in common and settled back into their old routine of talking about food and restaurants deep into the night when their shifts had ended.

What Gordon didn't know was that pressure had been building up in David's private life. He had borrowed £3,000 from the company just before leaving Scotland to sort out some financial difficulties. He was worried that he might be suffering from a recurrence of Hodgkin's disease, which he had fought off as a young man. And back in London other tensions were beginning to mount. A rash of resignations had hit the Gordon Ramsay restaurant since David had moved south and this was a nagging worry for Gordon, who prided himself on defying the critics and building long-term and loyal relationships with his staff. Matters came to a head in the late spring, when three female kitchen workers quit almost overnight. David's new regime was at issue, and something had to be done.

'Come on. We're off for something to eat,' Gordon told him. The two old mates headed for the super-chic restaurant on the top floor of Harvey Nichols in Knightsbridge to catch up and talk about the problem. While Gordon later said that David had seemed 'agitated and under pressure' at the start of the meal, he added that both of them had soon relaxed and the meeting had gone well. 'I said some staff members were not particularly happy with his style of management and we dealt with it immediately. David totally accepted responsibility and he spoke about the future.'

But the pair would never see each other again.

Within 24 hours of leaving the restaurant, David had climbed up some scaffolding, broken into an exclusive and well-guarded block of flats in Chelsea and started smashing windows with a golf club in a bizarre and random rage. He knew no one at the apartment building, had never been known to have visited it before and had no real reason even to have walked past it on the night in question. His presence there would be one of the many unsolved mysteries of the tragic evening.

Residents who tried to tackle the chef after calling the police said David wasn't violent when they approached him – but that he wasn't rational either. And for reasons that can never be explained he smashed yet another window, climbed through it on to the first of a series of ledges outside and tried to swing from a drainpipe on to the roof of a neighbouring building. At this point, he slipped and fell more than 50 feet on to the ground of the block's lower basement. Having suffered a broken neck and huge damage to his skull and back in the fall, David was pronounced dead by an ambulance crew at 12.54am. He was just 31.

'We've found a wallet. Can you come down with us to Horseferry Road and identify the body?' That's what Gordon remembers the police saying when they turned up at his restaurant the next day with the news of what had happened. In total shock, Gordon had to say no. 'I just couldn't do that,' he says. He asked his father-in-law, Chris, the company's finance director, to accompany the police instead. The entire staff at Gordon Ramsay then waited, tense and tearful, to hear if their absent head chef was indeed the man lying dead in the public mortuary in Westminster.

When they found out that it was, the whole company was in shock. 'David was the inspiration behind the launch of Amaryllis in Glasgow and went on to win Glasgow's only Michelin star. His loss will be felt by all of us who have worked with him,' the company said in its official statement on David's death.

Gordon himself went further. 'I am completely shocked and devastated by the news. David has worked for me for the past eight years and was not only a brilliant protege but also a friend. Everyone is deeply saddened by the loss of such a talented colleague. He was one of the most gifted Scottish chefs to ever work in my kitchen. He had remarkable grounding and great skills but also real vision, all of which combined to make him a natural leader and a great chef.' As a friend, Gordon said David had also been fiercely loyal and utterly protective. 'He was full-on, but if you were in the street and someone pushed you he would jump in. He wouldn't think twice about asking any questions. Losing him is such a huge waste of talent and energy.'

For Gordon and his colleagues, there were more shocks to come, however, most notably as medical details emerged about the manner in which David had died. Doctors said both alcohol and cocaine were present in David's blood on the night of his death, and that he had suffered a rare and bizarre reaction to the drug. The medical experts said David had suffered a psychotic response known as excited delirium – something that can occur whether you are a new or regular cocaine user and whether you take a large or small amount of the drug. 'The typical scenario is rapid onset of paranoia, followed by aggression towards objects, particularly glass,' the Westminster coroner, Dr Paul Knapman, said at David's inquest, before recording a verdict of accidental death.

Gordon, who had been called to speak at the inquest, was still trying to come to terms with the loss and with the news that his best friend, like his brother, had been a drug user. He was also trying to comfort and support David's previous partners, Fiona and Pauline, who were now having to raise the young chef's children on their own. Last but by no means least, Gordon was tormented by the fact that he should have been able to see that his friend was in trouble and should have been able to help him. 'It has been a tough, emotional six months and when you are close to someone, like I was with David, you do of course take on more responsibility. He was tremendous, we spent so much time together, but I never saw any signs that he had a problem with drugs. If I had, I would have sent him to rehab straight away. I do feel guilt and I am fighting

Family Man.
Top left: Gordon with his wife and four children. Away from the machismo of the kitchen, Gordon is a dedicated husband and father.

Top right: Gordon's marriage to Tana is bulletproof – they have stuck together through thick and thin.

Bottom: With baby daughter Megan at home in 1998.

Top: Chef Marco Pierre White (*left*) gave Gordon his first real break. Here they are pictured with critic and friend Michael Winner.

Bottom left: Gordon with his old friend and protégé Marcus Wareing at their restaurant, Petrus.

Bottom right: A man of many talents, Gordon is also very adept at swearing, whether it be verbally or, as pictured, by giving us the finger!

When Claridges became 'Gordon Ramsay at Claridges', the chef knew he was right at the top of his game. Here we see the restaurant's interior and Gordon in the kitchen where all the magic takes place.

Are the diners too fussy tonight?
BELINDA nice to see u smile tonight u were fab keep smiling
love SASHA x x x x x x x x x x x

SOUL FOOD
CATFISH
JAMBALAYA
BBQ RIBS
MOMMA CHERRI'S SOUL FOOD SHACK
HOTWINGS

Hell's Kitchen was an incredibly popular show. Amanda Barrie, pictured with comedian Al Murray (*top*) was one of its most emotional stars, and Edwina Currie (*bottom left*) gave a very memorable performance.

Bottom right: On *Ramsay's Kitchen Nightmares* Gordon made more friends than enemies. The biggest, brightest and most memorable of them turned out to be Charita Jones, the owner of Momma Cherri's Soul Food Shack.

Top left: Abi Titmuss brought a touch of glamour to *Hell's Kitchen*, and though Gordon sometimes snapped at her on the show, they remain friends.

Top right: Gordon was once ranked alongside Chris Evans and Mohamed Al Fayed as one of the worst people to work for in an ITV show called *Britain's Unbearable Bosses*.

Bottom: When he appeared on *Parkinson*, Gordon gave Ben Elton and Rod Stewart a taste of his famous £100 pizza. It is so expensive because of the shaved truffles used in the topping. The truffle here is worth over £1000.

Top left: Not known for mincing words, Gordon was happy to lay into shows such as *Can't Cook, Won't Cook* if they irritated him, as well as their hosts. Of Ainsley Harriot Gordon said he thought Ainsley's real ambition was not to be a top chef but to presen *Stars in their Eyes.* He questioned the method used by Gary Rhodes (*top right*)to produce chips in his kitchen, and famously described his former Stratford-upon-Avon neighbour Antony Worrall Thompson (*bottom left*) as 'a squashed Bee Gee'.

Bottom right: At one point, Gordon's wife frequently stocked up the family fridge with Jamie Oliver's ready meals from Sainsbury's – just to wind up her husband!

Top left: Gordon has produced numerous bestselling books. Here he is pictured at a signing for *Kitchen Heaven* in 2004.

Top right: Gordon picks up an award at *GQ* magazine's Man Of The Year.

Bottom left: Michael Winner and AA Gill. Gordon reckons he knows how to keep Winner happy – just keep the food coming. As for Gill, he once booted the critic out of his restaurant, whipping up a massive media storm in the process.

Bottom left: Gordon takes time out to show us how it's done at the Good Food Show in 2005.

Gordon has always kept up his interest in sport. He is pictured (*clockwise from top left*) with his medal at the London Marathon, taking part in the Volvo Ocean Race 2005, and running with Prince William at the London Sport Relief Mile.

internally as to why I couldn't spot it. If I'd done so, then maybe I could have stopped it from happening or attempted to stop it, put him in treatment. David had won his first Michelin star within seven months of starting at Amaryllis and he was thriving. He had a tremendous career in front of him…' Gordon's voice tailed off, and for once he was silent, overcome by the waste of a wonderful life and a true friend.

It was to be almost a year before he could bring himself to press the delete button on his mobile phone and erase the number of the man he had nicknamed Hector and with whom he had shared so much. And in that year the issue of drugs would come back to haunt him time and time again – normally at the behest of newspaper reporters. 'Since the news about David became public the tabloids have been crawling all over the place,' Gordon said sadly. 'One of my sommeliers has been offered money for a story – any story. Reporters have been rifling through the bins looking for drug-related paraphernalia. They're saying, "Is Gordon Ramsay pushing his chefs too far?" They want to find a problem and attack us for it.'

But Gordon and his company continued to be notoriously tough on drugs. 'We have zero tolerance of drugs and they do not enter any professional kitchen that we run. Anyone found taking any form of illegal substance would be immediately sacked.' He also said he was considering ways to introduce compulsory drug testing for new employees as part of their interview process – though legal restrictions ultimately made this a non-starter.

Other top chefs and industry sources lined up to say drugs were rife in restaurant kitchens, however. In the best-selling book *Kitchen Confidential*, Michelin-starred chef and self-confessed former drug user Anthony Bourdain told some hair-raising stories of the role drink and drugs played in professional kitchens. Then, shortly after David's death, an investigation by *Caterer and Hotelkeeper* claimed that many senior cooks actually encourage young staff to take drugs to help them deal with the hours and the high pressure. The magazine's survey of 1,000 hospitality workers also found that 40 per cent of respondents said they had seen colleagues take illegal drugs during working hours, while some 59 per cent said they had seen colleagues drink to excess while on duty in kitchens. A separate survey said a quarter of all accidents in professional kitchens were alcohol-related.

Meanwhile, a staggering 99 per cent of *Caterer and Hotelkeeper*'s respondents said they thought alcohol in particular was a problem for their industry, to which Peter Kay of the alcohol education charity the Ark Foundation said, 'The only thing that surprises me about that figure is what the other one per cent were thinking.' The Ark Foundation, set up by a former executive chef of the Ritz Hotel in London, was unequivocal in its stance. 'There is without doubt an alcohol and drug problem in this industry. The culture of the hard-drinking chef used to seem appealing. Now it needs to be addressed,' it declared.

Gordon, horrified that young people could risk throwing away their future by becoming addicted to drugs, was one of what felt like a minority of voices decrying the trend. Bob Cotton, chief executive of the British Hospitality Association, was among the few others who seemed to be on his side. 'Long hours are an excuse, not a reason for the rise in drug-taking. Lots of people work long hours and they don't take drugs,' said Cotton.

Gordon could not have agreed more and he revealed a surprisingly paternal attitude to his staff. 'People say you need drugs to provide the energy for this job. It's the biggest load of rubbish. The pressure does not drive anyone to having a dependency on chemicals. It does not drive anyone to taking coke. I'm sure there are drugs in the industry. But I don't smoke, I don't drink. I go to the gym three days a week and I run 40 miles. When I see young guys coming into my kitchen, I do fear for them but I say to them all, "If you're not here to enjoy it later in life, what's the point?"'

Tragically, while trying to win the hearts and minds of his colleagues and the catering industry, Gordon found out that he was losing the latest battle to save his brother. The man who had been spared a prison sentence a year ago, who had said he was clear of drugs and ready for a fresh start without them, had lapsed yet again. Unknown to Gordon, he was also in serious trouble with the police. He had been arrested for non-payment of past fines and breaking his probation order and sentenced to three months in prison in Exeter. And the first Gordon knew about it was when a newspaper reporter rang him to ask for a comment.

When he was released from prison, Ronnie got a job with a cross-Channel lorry firm based in Plymouth and in his regular phone calls to Gordon he said he was once more determined to settle down and stay off drugs. But Gordon got the shock of his life when the brothers finally met up for the first time in more than a year. The setting was hardly ideal. Gordon had just come back from a business trip to Australia and was working in the kitchens in London one Monday morning when the phone rang. His mother had been rushed to hospital after a suspected heart attack. Gordon dropped everything and drove to Somerset to see her.

By the time he arrived, Helen was on her way to making a full recovery and was sitting up in bed looking pretty good. The same could not be said of Ronnie. 'He was thin, gaunt, with black rings under his eyes and hunched shoulders, all shrivelled up like an old man,' Gordon says. And as they left the hospital Gordon knew he had to keep his distance once more. It would have been all too easy to believe his brother's promises, perhaps pay for a new course of detox or rehab, and hope that this time it would somehow be different. Instead, Gordon tried to harden his heart. He wished Ronnie luck and said goodbye. For once, the younger man would have to sink or swim.

Back in London, Gordon had enough new challenges to face. The good news was that his empire still seemed to be growing. Petrus had long since been an established part of London's fine-dining world and was about to move into a new home at the five-star Berkeley Hotel in Knightsbridge, where it would be joined by another Ramsay venture, the Boxwood Cafe. Meanwhile, Gordon's unofficial takeover of London's other luxury hotels was also gaining ground. He now had his eye on the dining rooms of the Savoy.

The Savoy Grill was one of the most formal and established of the capital's restaurants. Winston Churchill's favourite table, number four, had been left empty for a year after his death as a mark of respect. More recently, media figures such as Sir David Frost saw it as their home from home and it was equally popular with politicians and chief executives. While courting couples had sealed their love in the romantic setting of Gordon's original Aubergine, almost exclusively male FTSE 100 bosses sealed their billion-pound takeover bids at the Savoy. Tradition, discretion and reliability were its watchwords. Fine dining, however, had never been seen as much of a priority there. When he and Marcus Wareing took over the Savoy Grill, Gordon admitted he couldn't believe that such a famous, long-established restaurant had never been awarded a single Michelin star. He and Marcus changed that within a year – while retaining the faith, and the custom, of all the media, business and political figures who filled its tables.

So much activity helped Gordon take his mind off what had happened to David Dempsey and what was still happening to his brother. But it wasn't enough to blot out the other storms on the horizon. The first one broke when Gordon admitted his triumphant move back to Glasgow with Amaryllis had ended in failure. Stars including Kylie Minogue, Robbie Williams, Rod Stewart and Elton John had eaten at One Devonshire Gardens and the restaurant was packed almost every Friday and Saturday night, for which there was a six-week, 800-strong waiting list. The picture was very different on every other night of the week, however, when staff could almost outnumber diners. 'Opening a restaurant in Scotland was a dream and we got off to a phenomenal start with two years of great trading,' Gordon explains. 'But then it got a little bit more fancy, a little bit more pompous and customers were disappearing. I certainly learned a hell of a lot from it.'

He had also spent a hell of a lot on it. His company's figures showed the restaurant was losing around £200,000 a year, and Gordon calculated that in total he had lost £500,000 on the venture. So, however much it hurt his pride, he knew he had to pull the plug. 'Amaryllis was very dear to his heart and the decision was taken very reluctantly,' his spokeswoman said. The closure took immediate effect and caught everyone by surprise, among them Justin Timberlake, who had checked in to One Devonshire Gardens just days before. The singer was one of many people left looking for a new party venue when Amaryllis locked its doors for good.

Unfortunately, this wasn't the only Ramsay restaurant that wasn't going to live up to its hype. Shortly afterwards, complications over a lease and rumours of poor business would shut down Fleur, another London restaurant that Gordon had been linked to. And when that news broke the critics lined up to suggest the man himself could be in trouble.

At the start of 2004, the latest accounts showed the financial health of Gordon Ramsay Holdings had lurched into the red – from a £145,000 profit to a £1-million loss in just 12 months. A lawsuit from a former employee at Gordon's restaurant at the Connaught, who claimed that he had been forced to lift heavy weights while suffering from a hernia, added to a sudden rash of negative publicity and depressing headlines. So had Gordon spread himself too thinly, as many catering insiders had predicted? Was he trying to do too much, to prove too many points and win too many battles? If he was, the free advice handed out by a variety of newspaper pundits and columnists was that he should get back to basics. He was told to keep his head down, focus on the food and try to weather the storms.

But keeping a low profile in the late spring of 2004 was never going to be easy. The expletive-filled first episode of Channel 4's *Ramsay's Kitchen Nightmares* had made more waves than anyone had imagined. Overnight, Tim Gray, the unlucky chef from Bonaparte's, had become almost as famous as his foul-mouthed tormentor. And with the media frenzy over that first show refusing to die down, Gordon knew things were going to get a lot worse before they got better – because shouting down Tim Gray wasn't to be his only onscreen role that year. Over the next three weeks, the chefs at another clutch of nightmare restaurants were going to be seen taking his blows. And then an even bigger television project was set to begin.

TWELVE

NIGHTMARES AND ACCUSATIONS

The rancid scallops, unconventional omelettes and bad attitudes of Bonaparte's weren't the only horrors Gordon stumbled upon when he went out to film that first series of *Ramsay's Kitchen Nightmares*. And, fortunately for viewers, he was ready to tackle all the other disasters he saw in his usual brutal and uncompromising style. Critics said the next three shows in the series were 'difficult to watch, but impossible to turn off' because of Gordon's kill-or-cure, cook-eat-cook approach – and nearly five million viewers a week agreed. At the end of the series, the programme was credited with triggering ITV's 'Black Tuesday' – one of the worst ratings slumps in the channel's history as more than one viewer in five chose to watch Gordon over any other terrestrial or satellite programme.

In the process, 37-year-old Gordon found himself turning into an unlikely heart-throb. He had been horrified a couple of years earlier when a reporter wrote that he looked a decade older than he was and that he had the kind of face 'that you once saw long ago on young First World War soldiers returning old from the trenches'. So he kept having the blond streaks put in his hair, he kept doing his afternoon workouts at the near-empty gyms in his London hotels – and he kept showing off the results. His television directors loved the fact that he seemed willing to take his shirt off in front of the cameras and change clothes far more often than seemed strictly necessary for the job in hand. And, of course, they loved the fact that he continued to speak his mind about everything they put in front of him.

'Gordon needs to be handled with all the care of a truckload of nitro-glycerine,' a spokeswoman for Channel 4 admitted when asked about his temperament. Unfortunately for them, however, she didn't seem to have passed that warning on to Neil Farrell and Richard Collins at the Glass House restaurant in Ambleside, Cumbria. In 2004, this was to be the second restaurant featured in *Ramsay's Kitchen Nightmares*. And it would end up making almost as many headlines as the first.

In his defence, many of the problems at the Glass House were not of owner Neil's making. For example, the restaurant had opened just days before the foot-and-mouth crisis temporarily made much of the Lake District off limits. So his anticipated tourist trade wasn't able to get to his restaurant and the locals had a lot more on their minds than trying out his unique garlic popcorn. With a frightening VAT bill outstanding and too many empty tables in the evenings, Neil was at crisis point. So he reckoned he had nothing to lose by calling in the cameras. 'I felt I had already been to hell and back, so why not invite Mr Hell himself?' he said of Gordon.

And Mr Ramsay turned into Mr Hell within hours of arriving at the restaurant for the ten-day assessment and advice period. Having ordered two deep-fried duck cakes, Gordon was presented with what he described as 'something looking like a pair of camel's bollocks. A pair of dried camel's bollocks.' And worse was to come when he bit into the restaurant's signature dish, nearly broke a tooth and then choked on a bone. Having been watching what else went on in the kitchen, Gordon was ready to let rip with some of his favourite language. 'Some idle mother fucker had been too lazy to bone the duck properly. Then the dozy twat accuses me of planting the fucking bone. Then he started to make pesto. He ran out of pine nuts so he says, "Just stuff in almonds, the punters won't know." So he starts walloping in almonds. Then the fucking owner says my Caesar salad is crap. We are in the middle of service and he is fucking ranting on. So I tell him to fuck off.'

Which is when things got even more heated. 'What happens next is I let rip,' Gordon told Olga Craig of the *Sunday Telegraph* afterwards. 'One hundred and eleven fucks worth of rip. I mullered him. We came close to blows.' The squaring-up happened in the courtyard behind the kitchens, and production company staff ultimately kept the two from getting too physical. But the verbal battering went on. Head chef Richard Collins was close to tears most of the time and one of the kitchen porters with a phobia about raw fish was teased by Gordon so much that he quit.

Once more, it was great, passionate television. But, once more, some serious advice came as soon as the expletive-laden assessment period was over. And this time some worrying allegations were made as soon as the show was broadcast.

On the advice front, before the staff at the Glass House did anything else, Gordon demanded a massive clean-up of the kitchen. While the Ambleside restaurant had one of the cleaner kitchens he saw, he says a lack of basic hygiene was what shocked him the most about many of the others visited when researching and making *Ramsay's Kitchen Nightmares*. 'I was horrified, genuinely appalled by the standards I found.' And, apart from the clear health risks in some restaurants, he said he couldn't understand how chefs could have pride in their food and their profession when they were surrounded by rotting ingredients and grime.

Back at the Glass House, Gordon then argued that the menu Neil and Richard were offering was too long, too confusing and too unfocused for their target market. Do people who eat in country restaurants really need to pick from up to 90 different dishes at dinner? Gordon reckoned diners, the waiting staff and the chefs were all being overwhelmed by the vast amount of choice and suggested offering just six starters, six main courses and up to six puddings in the evenings. In typical fashion, he said they should also go for a simpler, fresher lunch menu of healthy open sandwiches. Inside the kitchen, Gordon reckoned he had found some real gems among the junior staff – and, as usual, he was keen to encourage them to step forward and make the most of their potential. Unfortunately, he reckoned that they could do so only if Neil sacked his

£25,000-a-year, Claridge's-trained head chef Richard – something the owner threatened but never quite managed to do.

So does Gordon turn the Glass House around? The food is simpler, the kitchen staff are happier and the takings are up by a fifth when he returns to check on progress. But when the show is finally broadcast Neil has plenty to say about what happened – or didn't happen – when the cameras had stopped rolling.

He accused Gordon and the producers of misleading him about the ultimate title of the series and refusing to let him see an advance copy of the show – a claim also made by Sue Ray of Bonaparte's. And he says they also hyped up and exaggerated his financial situation to create a false sense of tension for the show. 'Gordon Ramsay did a voice-over at the start of the programme and said I was in so much financial difficulty I had turned off my phone because I was being hounded by suppliers. But that was untrue. The reason I had turned it off was simply that I was with my family. I had told the production team that I don't want to be disturbed at home. It had nothing to do with suppliers and I am not in any financial difficulty.'

Neil also raised doubts about the real reason why Gordon had been so keen for him to ditch his head chef – a man praised in *The Good Food Guide* for his 'dazzling' desserts and 'clever' use of wine while at the pre-Ramsay Claridge's. In Neil's view, the chef had simply been a ratings-boosting scapegoat. 'They carefully edited the programme and portrayed the head chef as the weak link. But he and Gordon got on very well together. There was never a cross word between them off camera. I had no intention of sacking Richard but it would have made good television. And that is the only reason they wanted me to do it.'

Gordon, of course, stood firm and continued to argue his case in characteristically blunt language. 'He's a slob who lacks inspiration. If I had a fat, lazy head chef like that who couldn't cook for toffee, I would sell up and get out of the business,' was his final word on the subject.

Neil, however, hadn't finished. 'As far as I am concerned, the whole thing is about making Gordon Ramsay look good,' he said of the show. 'I admire his ability as a chef, but as a person not at all. The whole thing was a nightmare and I couldn't wait for him to go. We wanted to be on the show because we reckoned we had nothing to lose and I wanted to have Gordon Ramsay in my kitchen. But if I had known they had a pre-set agenda I would have had nothing to do with it.'

Media analyst Dr Cynthia McVey, who has spent years studying the reality-television phenomenon, said it is increasingly common for people to be angry after seeing themselves on the small screen. 'People want to take part because they are genuinely excited about being on television. They may even see it as a path to stardom, but when people see the result it can be very different. People think they have control and then they find that they don't.'

Wresting control back from Gordon Ramsay was something one other restaurateur tried to do in that first record-breaking series of *Ramsay's Kitchen Nightmares*. 'You have to find the courage to confront him,' said Francesco Mattioli, the new owner of the formerly celebrated restaurant the Walnut Tree, in South Wales, who disagreed with almost all of Gordon's advice. 'He can bombard you. Your head spins. But in the end I retaliated. I have great admiration for Gordon, but, let's put it this way, he was doing his programme. This is my restaurant. I don't take that rubbish from anybody.'

Gordon, of course, refused to accept that anyone could ignore his advice. When he came back to the Walnut Tree to check on progress, he found that Francesco hadn't spruced up the menu, hadn't cut prices and wasn't performing much better. And, after trying to get his message across one more time, another big row developed. 'I'll fuck off home and you can continue struggling. Let's leave it like that, you stubborn fucker,' were Gordon's final words before he did as he had promised.

As it turned out, the Walnut Tree wasn't the only restaurant that Gordon couldn't wait to rush away from as soon as the cameras had stopped filming. 'The title of the series, *Ramsay's Kitchen Nightmares*, was absolutely right. I still have recurring nightmares of some of the situations we encountered. I was mortified, really shocked on the customers' behalf, because you should never, in a professional kitchen, take a customer for granted. It was all a big eye-opener for me.' The bad attitudes he had first seen at Bonaparte's seemed to have made the most impression on him. But the words he used to describe what he had seen there could usefully be applied to other failing restaurants across the country. 'I find it hard to come to terms with people portraying themselves as senior chefs who clearly aren't and putting people's livelihoods at risk in the process. I didn't think it was possible for chefs to be so far up their own arses that they are totally oblivious to what the customers want, and so focused on satisfying their own egos that they are cooking what they wanted in the type of place where nobody wanted that sort of food. And, even if the customers had wanted it, some of these chefs didn't actually have a clue how to cook it.'

What also appalled the famously hard-working, early-starting Gordon was the short hours that many of the out-of-town chefs seemed prepared to put in. 'I discovered that too many of them roll into work at 10.30. But how the hell can you contemplate creating something special when you don't get to your kitchen till then?' he asked, genuinely amazed. 'I had a work ethic forced into me from the very first time I worked in a professional kitchen. I learned that you can't do this job with half your mind. That's what seems hardest to get across to some of the tossers who think it might be glamorous and social to run a restaurant. It isn't. It's hard fucking work day in and day out and I can't believe how many people haven't woken up to that yet.'

So would he film another series of the show? 'When I was first asked about a second series, I said I didn't know if I could do that to my fucking palate. I value that like there's no tomorrow. It used to be my left foot that I treasured and now it's my tongue.' But as it turned out Gordon decided his taste buds could survive another battering and he agreed to go back on the road for a new series of *Ramsay's Kitchen Nightmares* to be broadcast in 2005. But before then he had an even higher-profile, higher-pressure challenge to face. It was time for him to enter *Hell's Kitchen.*

THIRTEEN

WELCOME TO HELL'S KITCHEN

'We're going to be running a sophisticated venue, not a burger van on the A3. We won't be cooking fish and chips, steak and ale pie or a nut fucking risotto. It's going to be fine dining, exclusive, the best restaurant in London for two weeks.' Gordon certainly had the highest of hopes for *Hell's Kitchen*.

Television production companies had been deluging him with programme ideas ever since *Boiling Point* more than five years earlier. And, as the reality-television boom gathered momentum, they were keener than ever to find a way to use 'the ogre at the Aga' – one of the few men in Britain who could always be relied upon to speak his mind. But what kind of show should they make?

Gordon and fellow chefs like Marcus Wareing and Mark Sargeant would often bounce ideas between them after their long restaurant shifts had ended. And Gordon in particular had been keen to come up with something more serious than a standard celebrity-based reality show. Two key thoughts kept going round and round in his mind during these late-night conversations. One was of his own life story: the boy from nowhere who had been turned into an award-winning chef. The other was of Ed Devlin, the *Faking It* contestant who had also gone from zero to hero and proved himself as an effective and convincing head chef after just a few weeks of intensive instruction.

So could Gordon recreate those sorts of transformations on a far larger scale? Could he teach a group of people how to cook and run a top-quality restaurant in a matter of weeks? He decided he would like to have a go – and the production company Granada International decided to put up the money and let him.

The ultimate idea behind *Hell's Kitchen* turned out to be almost as simple as Gordon's initial late-night musings. While cameras watched every move, ten celebrities with little or no experience of cooking would go on a culinary boot camp with him. He would try to pass on a career's worth of information and knowledge so they could create meals fit for a Michelin star. And they would serve them in a specially created restaurant where real diners would be expecting the very best.

Getting a project like this up and running was going to take a huge amount of time, effort, money and planning. 'Viewers normally have no idea just how much goes on behind the scenes on shows like these,' says television production manager Alison Sheppard, who has worked on major reality shows for ITV and Sky One. 'You can often summarise the show in a couple of sentences but the actual logistics of turning those words into reality are terrifying. With something like *Hell's Kitchen*, where the contestants are effectively on set 24 hours a day, you need a really strong team of planners to consider every eventuality. And you really need to get the contestants and the other onscreen players right.'

Early on, Gordon decided to keep his side of the show in-house. He wanted Angela Hartnett and Mark Sargeant, two of his longest-standing colleagues, to come on board to help train up the contestants, though Angela in particular wasn't keen. 'It could have opened us up to a lot of criticism and in the first place I didn't want to do it,' she says.

But in the end both chefs were won over by Gordon's enthusiasm. 'I pretty much knew Gordon wouldn't dive into anything that was wrong,' said Mark. 'The big scare about this was: "Oh my God, it's a reality show." But this was so different. You weren't just sitting around doing nothing waiting for someone to have sex. It was about running a proper restaurant and that was exactly what we did. There was no set-up. No farce. It was real.'

The next challenge was deciding which celebrities should be Gordon's guinea pigs. 'You need to walk a dangerous tightrope here,' says Sheppard. 'You need people who are soft enough in some ways so viewers get to like them, but hard enough to create some tension and some controversy as well. You need some of them to be opinionated, some of them to be a little bit wild, you need plenty of sex appeal and as much baggage as you can get into the room. A little bitchiness doesn't normally go amiss either.' Fortunately, former MP Edwina Currie was ready to provide that from the start when she ran through a list of her fellow chefs. 'In all there were three actors, two singers, a comic, a disc jockey, an ex-Olympic runner and me. Oh yes, and Abi Titmuss,' she said disparagingly.

Gordon was hoping that among that mixed bunch there would also be someone else – a great chef. But finding them sounded like it would be a painful, gruesome process. 'If people take my advice and put away their own egos, we could have a magical kitchen. I'll strip away everything they know then build them up from scratch and discover their inner strengths. Among the ten, I know that there will be a naturally gifted cook, a real surprise. I want to show them the blood, sweat and tears that go into creating memorable food – and the drama of day-to-day life in a kitchen. I want them all to get turned on to the passion of cooking, to smell the fragrance of herbs, to see a pan of live young eels jumping, to chop liver, remove a pigeon's heart, disembowel a prawn, put a knife through a live lobster.'

It was starting to sound a lot like the worst bush-tucker trials in *I'm A Celebrity … Get Me Out Of Here!* And as the celebrities arrived for the first day of training Gordon finally admitted he was nervous. Nervous as in terrified.

'I'm crapping myself,' he admitted. 'There is a lot resting on it for me, not just because I've got three Michelin stars, but because the show is going to be live. I don't really know what I have let myself in for. This is turning out to be one of the most daunting tasks I have ever had. We have ten individuals and fifteen days, so we don't really have any excuse to fail. But I am already having nightmares about it.' He also had low expectations of the behaviour he could expect from the celebrities – and typically forthright, if illegal, ideas of how he would deal with it. 'I expect to encounter laziness, lack of ability and bad attitude every day. I don't expect to be questioned and, if anyone rubs me up the wrong way, they're going to get pummelled. They'll have their backsides seared on the charcoal grill. I'll brand them – criss-cross their butt on the burner.'

Unaware of the painful threat that was hanging over them, the whole group got together for the first time at Ealing, Hammersmith and West London College's restaurant Taste – coincidentally, the place where Jamie Oliver had recently filmed the far more critically acclaimed *Jamie's Kitchen*, of which more later. The ten celebrities were having their first few days of back-to-basics, preparatory training in the student kitchens and they were the exact mixed bunch that Sheppard had predicted. Gordon stood back and looked at them, the frown lines on his forehead even deeper than usual.

Alongside Edwina Currie and Abi Titmuss stood the three actors, *Gimme Gimme Gimme* star James Dreyfus and Amanda Barrie and Jennifer Ellison, formerly of *Coronation Street* and *Brookside* respectively. The two singers were Belinda Carlisle and Matt Goss from Bros. The 'Pub Landlord' comedian Al Murray was standing next to controversial former sprinter Dwain Chambers. The veteran investigative journalist Roger Cook was the last of the group, though after falling and injuring himself during the initial cooking lessons he was replaced by the equally veteran DJ Tommy Vance.

Gordon's first task was to explain how tough things were going to be. 'You will have to sweep the floor ten times an hour, peel a bucket of onions, cook for the staff. You will also scrub clean your own pans because this stops you from burning things. You'll be amazed how careful chefs are if they know they have to scrape the burned gunk off the bottom of their own saucepans. I don't give a damn about diplomacy or delicacy. The more honest I am with you the better you will become.'

One noticeable thing about Gordon's opening speeches to the team was the relative lack of swearing. When he laid out the ground rules, he kept his language pretty clean. But anyone who thought he had changed his ways was in for a shock. The effing and blinding was back the moment the celebrities cooked their signature dishes for his analysis. And it wouldn't go away. When the final count was done, broadcasting authorities said there had been just over 5,000 swear words in the show – almost all of them from Gordon.

Back in the calm before the storm, Gordon introduced the celebrities to his co-chefs, Angela and Mark. They would head up the blue and red teams, which would compete against each other as the early skills of food preparation were learned and the first real meals were cooked. And, after the first few days of training, as the teams got ready for the pressure of pulling off a real restaurant service, Gordon was convinced that everything was going to go well. 'If the celebrities were soppy and a little bit up their own arse, then I would be concerned,' he said, when asked about his early impressions. 'But they are so eager. They are starting to come to terms with the pressure valve and the highs and lows that go on in the kitchen. I really think they'll get into fifth gear when they need to.'

Unfortunately, storm clouds were already building up on the horizon. ITV had constructed a massive, purpose-built kitchen and restaurant in London's East End for the main part of the show. It was sited just off the increasingly trendy Brick Lane, more famous for its curries and lagers than for its fine dining. And, by the time the celebrities arrived there, several of them had long since become fed up with the boring, repetitious nature of their early tasks. They were also tired of all the standing up, disoriented by the heat and increasingly angered by Gordon's perfectionist demands. Mistakes were made, tensions were mounting – and when Dwain Chambers nearly sliced off his finger with a knife the first drops of blood were spilled. It was turning into *Hell's Kitchen* indeed.

What some of the television critics – and the celebrities – said at this point was that Gordon was pushing everyone too hard, shouting too loud, asking too much and playing up for the camera at every opportunity. But he refused to compromise or apologise.

'Everyone was being paid a fortune to be on that show, so I wasn't going to allow anyone to think they didn't have to work,' he said when asked to justify his tough stance afterwards. 'This show is not about celebrity status and all I am concerned about is their cooking ability or the lack of it. I had seen from day one that they were all out to launch their biographies, careers, CDs, whatever it is, but I wasn't taking any of it. They are not celebrities on this show and I am not a celebrity chef. I'm a fucking chef. Period. I don't have a long shot, a wide shot and three times to rehearse the fucking Gordon Ramsay pastry. Everything I do is natural. It's live. It's me.'

The one allowance Gordon did make for the celebrities in his charge was that they were like fish out of water in the kitchen – and that he could just about remember how that had felt himself. 'There are two sides to me when I deal with them all. There is the ugly monster that craves perfection and then there is the other individual who understands what they are going through. I can understand because I've done what they are doing now. I was in love with football, but I had to find something else and work at it. I know how hard it is to start again.'

Gordon's fellow chefs also made the point that his high-profile pupils were hardly shrinking violets who needed to be handled with kid gloves. 'All of these celebrities are people who have succeeded in their own fields; they are not people who do things lightly. They are in a situation where they are no longer top dog and they are going through emotional turmoil; they are going through hell, but that is what a kitchen is really like,' said Marcus Wareing.

Mark Sargeant also pointed out that the trainees should be able to see through Gordon's rages and appreciate how desperately he wanted to inspire them. 'If he reduces someone to tears, it is not because he has just decided to pick on you. Half the time the people are crying because they know he is right. If you weren't learning and there wasn't a flip-side to it, then no one would be interested. But, while the bad side is very bad, the good side is fantastic and that's why he can make people cry but gain their loyalty in the end.'

A small number of outsiders also argued that Gordon was being more constructive than many critics thought.

'His full-frontal aggression is as shocking as a smack and if Ramsay used it in the unpredictable manner of a bully it would diminish him as all bullies are essentially weak. But he wields it only to sharpen people up and get the job done,' wrote journalist Colette Douglas Home in the *Daily Mail*. And a closer analysis showed there was a lot more to Gordon's dialogue than an endless stream of swearing. When he tried to describe the texture, colour, taste, appearance and potential of food, there were flashes of real sensitivity and passion in his language. He was desperate to communicate his own feelings for food to the others and there was real poetry in his praise when the trainee chefs did make progress.

And progress was very important because the clock was ticking and the temporary restaurant's first diners were about to take their seats on the other side of the kitchen wall. One of the extra ingredients which made *Hell's Kitchen* work was the contrast between the crises in the kitchens and the rubber-necking that could go on in the main dining room when the evening's guests arrived. While it may not always have seemed exactly like the hottest ticket in town – the celebrity levels rarely rose above the B-list – the comings and goings of the diners themselves made great television. Angus Deayton had bounced back from being sacked from *Have I Got News For You?* after a series of newspaper revelations about his private life and was interviewing the diners as they ate. Or, more often, as they waited to eat.

On the first day that Gordon and his celebrities attempted to cook for a full restaurant, just 32 of the 72 diners were served a meal. The late Mo Mowlam left to buy a curry in Brick Lane after waiting two hours for her main course. Even more embarrassing for Gordon was when rival chef Antony Worrall Thompson also gave in to hunger and left the restaurant to try to find food elsewhere. 'They can't cope,' he said of Gordon and his team as he left.

Royal correspondents Jennie Bond and Nicholas Owen were also seen going hungry, while comedian Vic Reeves told Deayton that Gordon had 'taken umbrage' when he had asked for egg and chips. 'I don't know what his problem is. It was quite a simple order,' he said sarcastically. Throw the arrival of some newspaper food critics – or 'fucking food critics' as Gordon preferred to call them – and the tension could hardly get higher.

'Disgrace. Fucking disgrace. Fucking ashamed of ourselves. Fucking awful performance. Fucking pissed off' was his considered opinion of the night. And things didn't get better very quickly. Over the next few days, arguments in the kitchen got even worse as the celebrities tried to please Gordon and their other mentors in the day and serve all their customers in the evening. What made matters even harder for everyone was that Gordon was starting to feel the pressure of running all his restaurants and fitting in all his other business and family responsibilities.

He would start at Claridge's at 7am most mornings, spend the day shuttling between it, his other kitchens and *Hell's Kitchen* and end up back at Claridge's around 1.45am to catch up on the day. On the short break between the initial training of the celebrities in west London and the move to the East End, he fitted in a trip to New Zealand to work on an international scholarship he had set up for young chefs three years earlier, and his publishers wanted him to do a jet-lag-inducing one-day book-signing trip to New York to promote *Kitchen Heaven* as well. His famously short temper was even more frayed than normal – though his sense of humour and his ability to be politically incorrect remained as strong as ever. 'I'm so stressed I'm having nightmares again,' he said as the pressure mounted. 'I woke up in a cold sweat at 6.30am this morning having a nightmare about Edwina in the nude. I was like, Fucking hell, this is not a good image.'

While she was seeing even less of her husband than normal during the filming of the show, Tana was convinced he would last the pace. 'Gordon likes the challenge of it all and he went into it with his eyes open. It is frustrating, it is tough and I feel for him, but this is what he thrives on.'

As it turned out, the same could not be said for all of the celebrities. Mutiny had been in the air ever since the training sessions had ended and the real work had begun. At 26, Dwain Chambers was one of the youngest on the show and as an ex-athlete he was one of the fittest. But even he found the physical and mental demands of keeping up with Gordon too much and so he quit after one row too many. 'It's too tough,' he said afterwards. 'It was an experience but it was not fun. It's hot, it's stressful, there's a lot of verbal, you end up swearing yourself and I'm not a guy who likes to swear. We all got cuts and bruises, it was hard as hell and I'm just glad I'm out.'

Tommy Vance left the same day – refusing to attend the morning roll-call to tell Gordon that he was going. As a former worker in the Merchant Navy's catering corps, 63-year-old Tommy had been expected to fare better than his less experienced colleagues. But he lasted just 36 hours on the show after finding the atmosphere too poisonous and the 100-degree heat in the kitchen too much to bear. Meanwhile, the increasingly tearful pair of Amanda Barrie and James Dreyfus threatened to follow their former colleagues amid talk of a mass walkout by all the celebrities.

More worryingly for Gordon – and for ITV – was the fact that some two million viewers had also given up on *Hell's Kitchen*. The first show drew seven million viewers on the opening Sunday night, a figure which rose two nights later to an impressive 8.3 million, or one in three people watching TV. But by the middle of that first week the viewing figures had slumped by more than three million. 'Gordon Ramsay has always claimed that he hates being called a celebrity chef. Well, he's about to find out how it feels to be called a former celebrity chef,' wrote one columnist as the vultures gathered around the show.

The television critics were particularly savage. 'It's like a restaurant version of *I'm A Celebrity ... Get Me Out Of Here!* without the inconvenience and expense of having to ship everybody to Australia. It's like *Big Brother* in a kitchen or *Survivor* without the sand. It's that same, clapped-out formula all over again but this time to the background of pots and pans and with the ringmaster in a chef's white jacket,' wrote the *Daily Mail*'s Neil Lyndon, who said the show could be the final nail in the coffin for reality television in general. 'It certainly looks as if our appetite might be sated for watching Gordon Ramsay berating his hapless victims with all the guttersnipe incoherence and foul-mouthed boorishness of David Beckham reviling a linesman. Once is more than enough for this experience. Every night is unendurable.'

What hurt Gordon even more was the fact that one of his original mentors also felt he had to speak out against the show and his part in it. 'I don't believe that food and cooking should be treated in this way,' said Michel Roux, the grand old man of British cooking, who had been Gordon's hero at Le Gavroche nearly two decades earlier. 'I don't blame Gordon, he is the flavour of the day and he is using his situation to feed a want. But it is a sad thing. Years ago, we couldn't talk about food or sex in this country, now everyone is an expert and everyone wants to see a top chef and Gordon is the best we have. But food is being trivialised and treated like a joke.'

Jan Moir, the award-winning restaurant critic of the *Daily Telegraph*, was equally concerned about the message the show was sending out and she had her own theory about what was behind it all. 'You have to ask what the point of it all is. Gordon is so much above his rivals, he is in a league of his own. What he has done with his restaurants is incredible, but I think *Hell's Kitchen* is going to be a disaster. The show is going to America and I wonder if that is what it is all about. I just hope Gordon does not become an Anne Robinson figure.'

It turned out that some of Gordon's bosses were equally concerned. 'The new owners of Claridge's are worried that Gordon being in a reality-television series and all his swearing is too downmarket for the brand. Claridge's success is based on its upmarket image and although it is becoming more modern this TV series is going too far,' the *Daily Mail* was told, while Martyn Nail, executive head chef at one of the hotel's other restaurants, said Gordon's new incarnation as the bad boy of television cooking made his employers 'incredibly nervous'.

At one point, it seemed as if even Hollywood stars were ganging up on him. When Sharon Stone was staying at Claridge's to promote her latest film, *Catwoman*, she saw a photo of the hotel's head chef on the wall outside his restaurant. 'Who is he?' she asked her minder. 'Oh, I see, he's a reality-television star,' she summed up after hearing a run-though of his recent achievements.

But even more worrying for Gordon was the fact that it wasn't just the experts, his peers or film stars who were confused or disappointed with his show. The *Sun*'s letters pages are not always the place for the most considered of opinions. But few can really argue with those of reader Margaret Campbell, who wrote in during the first week of the show. 'I can't help but think Gordon Ramsay's ITV series *Hell's Kitchen* is a waste of money compared to the similar *Jamie's Kitchen* on Channel 4,' she wrote. 'Loads of food is thrown away and wasted in *Hell's Kitchen* and the celebrity contestants aren't even interested in getting a kitchen job. Jamie Oliver's series got unemployed youngsters off the streets and gave them the opportunity to train for a new career and start a new life, which seems far more worthwhile to me.'

Heading home in the early hours after yet another bad night in Brick Lane, Gordon couldn't hide his fears. After so many years of hard-fought success, had he risked everything and utterly misjudged the public mood? As a boy, he had sworn he would never cry in front of his father. Now he knew he risked being humiliated in front of the whole country. Could this be the high-profile public failure that he had spent a lifetime trying to avoid?

FOURTEEN

GORDON VERSUS EDWINA

Singer and former *Brookside* babe Jennifer Ellison would ultimately become the winner of *Hell's Kitchen* and be crowned Top Celebrity Chef. But the grand old ladies Edwina Currie and Amanda Barrie would prove to be the real celebrity stars of the show. And Abi Titmuss was to save it from a ratings disaster.

Abi's unwitting role in the drama came after a series of bad nights in the restaurant and bad training sessions in the kitchens. Gordon was becoming increasingly fraught and frustrated – and he vented his anger on Abi, the former nurse who was turning herself into a media personality after dating the troubled television host John Leslie.

'Every time I look around you're fucking giggling. This is fucking serious. We are so fucking close to getting it spot on and you think this is a fucking joke.' Written out here, the words don't look too awful, at least by Gordon's famously aggressive standards. But in reality they were simply the start of a 60-second-plus diatribe that was almost unprecedented in its ferocity. And they were delivered with the chef's face just inches from that of his victim.

After trying to justify herself and apologise, Abi, not surprisingly, ended up temporarily leaving the set and collapsing in tears. It was a turning point for the show, with Gordon accused of extreme sexism and of crossing the line between acceptable and unacceptable behaviour. But it got people watching again.

As the second week approached, viewing figures suddenly picked up and on the crucial Sunday night when it went head to head with the first show of that year's *Big Brother* it was more than one million ahead in the ratings. The following night *Hell's Kitchen* had almost twice as many viewers as Nadia, Ahmed, Victor and their other new housemates. In one sense, professional disaster for Gordon looked as if it had been averted. But the on-set battles were only just beginning.

Strip-club boss Peter Stringfellow was one of the restaurant's hopeful diners on the night Gordon launched his verbal attack on Abi. And he had characteristically blunt advice for the wannabe glamour girl. 'Go on, girl – hit him,' he said after seeing the pair together. But while Abi held back, Amanda Barrie was to prove a whole lot less restrained.

Carry On Cleo's Amanda, who had become one of ITV's *Bad Girls* after her long stint in *Coronation Street*, says it all began after a particularly sleepless night in the celebrities' accommodation block. Everyone had been up until 4am celebrating Jennifer's 21st birthday; Matt had played guitar and the others had tried to sing, with varying degrees of success. They were then back in the kitchen with Gordon at 8am. 'Gordon was about to tell me what disgusting bit of dead animal I was going to have to deal with that morning, but before he began I suddenly thought I was going to be sick and pass out. I asked to be excused and dashed off screen, where the nurse insisted on taking my blood pressure. Gordon followed me and, despite it being obvious that I felt absolutely wretched, proceeded to shout and scream at me and accuse me of spoiling everything and trying to get out of working. The reality was that I was desperate not to be sick on camera. I was furious with him. Luckily, my blood pressure was all right and after drinking some water I went back to work.'

No one's blood pressure stayed low for long, however. 'An hour or so later, I was asked to collect a heavy box of apples from the walk-in fridge freezer,' Amanda continues. 'I had been complaining for three days that the light didn't work in there. It was very dark, the floor was a skating rink and very dangerous. I had asked if someone could do something about it. They hadn't, so inevitably I slipped and fell. I didn't hurt myself but again I went out and asked for a light to be fitted to stop someone else from breaking their neck. Outside, instead of listening to me, Gordon said he wanted to discuss speciality dishes.'

Which was when it all kicked off. 'I just saw red and took a swipe at him. He grabbed my arms very firmly and shouted, "Don't raise your hand at me." He was pretty strong – all that chopping has given him powerful arm muscles – but all I thought was, I missed you the first time, you silly little man, but I won't again. In all, I am told I tried to whack him five times. He started to grapple with me, then shouted for security, who turned up and prised us apart.'

It was at this point that Amanda says she lost respect for the chef. 'What kind of 37-year-old man calls for outside help to deal with a 68-year-old woman? Am I so intimidating and strong? Where is his dignity?' she asked afterwards, appalled.

The next morning after roll-call, Amanda decided that she too should follow Dwain and Tommy and quit the show. 'When I took a swipe at you yesterday, quite honestly I thought, I'm totally out of control here and I am obviously not in control of myself when I am around you. I am either in tears or taking a whack at you and that is no way to behave,' she told the exhausted-looking Gordon as she resigned from her post. 'It has been quite an experience but I think I would like to go home now and watch the rest of the show in bed with a bottle of Champagne and some fish and chips.'

Gordon took the news calmly. 'Amanda, I admire your honesty and thank you,' he said. 'And can I just say it was a bloody good shot.'

Losing Amanda did not lower the tensions, however, because *Hell's Kitchen* had just entered a new phase. Contestants were now being voted off the show in a nightly public vote, with a tearful Belinda Carlisle first to go. 'I am happy to go home and see my family but in other ways I am sad to leave,' the singer told Angus Deayton in a post-eviction interview. 'I love to cook but not to that level,' she said. And as she left the set she gave Gordon a rare compliment. 'He is great and it is never personal,' she concluded when asked about his rantings.

Firmly back in the real world, Belinda's former confidante and red-team mate Amanda was less flattering about their former teacher and the whole structure of the show. 'Anyone – myself included – who is silly enough to go into one of these reality shows deserves everything they get. And anyone who goes into the kitchen with Gordon Ramsay should know exactly what they are letting themselves in for,' she began. 'I half-admire him as a showman and recognise that he can be charismatic but he is also a typical bully and when he becomes deliberately, personally cruel it is offensive and deeply unfunny. He has developed a technique of alternately praising you, then knocking you down so you don't know where you are. In the end you are so pleased not to be browbeaten that you become totally placid.'

Others were also lining up to call the former footballer the biggest drama queen on television. Dr Patrick Tissington of Aston Business School has spent much of his career analysing how people function in the high-pressure worlds of the Armed Forces, the Royal Marines and the emergency services. And he wasn't convinced Gordon was coping. 'Too much time and emotional effort is expended on confrontation rather than in getting the job done,' he said. 'Ramsay would be dismissed as "a flapper" by fire officers or others who have to make life-and-death decisions under pressure.'

When it came to teaching the celebrities, other professionals said he was getting it right, however. 'Gordon is not the bullying one-trick pony he has been accused of being,' said Jonathan Cormack, a consultant at human resources giant the Hay Group. 'If you look carefully you see he is always encouraging the chef to pass on tips and expertise and he asks questions of his staff that show he is trying to understand what motivates them.'

'He lets people make their own mistakes and then pulls them up for it. It may look horrible at times but it is effective,' added occupational psychologist Marc Atherton.

But was everything that viewers saw on their screens a true depiction of life on set? Having spent her post-eviction hours reviewing some of the tapes, Amanda said most of what she had seen bore no resemblance to reality. Her biggest gripe was that, while the celebrities were in the kitchen from 8am to 4pm before having an hour's break and then working from 5pm until midnight, the same could not be said of Gordon. 'He is always presented as if he is tough, in control and in the kitchen all the time when he was only there three or four hours a day. The rest of the time it is left to his henchmen, Mark Sergeant and Angela Hartnett. No wonder he had all that energy to scream and shout when he did appear,' she said.

Amanda also claimed clever editing had dramatically affected the way the events and the various personalities were presented. 'The producers put what they want the audience to see on the screen, rather than what is actually happening. And that includes showing Ramsay in a very good light. No one saw what led up to me losing my temper. Instead, I was made to look like a mad old woman who couldn't cope. I was made to look 98 instead of 68,' she said of her infamous punch-up with Gordon.

She claimed the editors and producers were equally cruel about how they portrayed most of the other celebrities. 'Belinda was shown as a snivelling wreck but she is a highly intelligent woman and one of the best cooks there. And Matt Goss was made to look entirely placid when in fact he is hilariously funny and kind. Abi, meanwhile, was made to look angelic when in reality she talked dirty about sex almost non-stop. I am as broadminded as they get, but there is a line to draw and she was disgusting. Edwina, meanwhile, is made to appear selfish in the programme whereas in reality she was like a mother to us all.'

Well, she was like a mother to everyone except Gordon.

What was dubbed 'The Edwina and Gordon Show' became one of the other gripping and most memorable elements of the series. It had been an inspired idea to put someone as famously forthright as the former Cabinet Minister Edwina Currie into *Hell's Kitchen* – with an extra culinary frisson coming from the fact that she had triggered a financial crisis in the food industry and been forced to resign as Health Minister in 1988 after saying most of the country's egg production was infected with salmonella. Having left Parliament and reinvented herself as a best-selling novelist, she had stormed back into the public eye in 2002 after it was revealed that she had had a two-year affair with the famously grey former Prime Minister John Major – an affair he later described as 'the most shameful event' of his life.

From the start, Edwina was ready to admit that she knew next to nothing about cooking. 'I thought aspic was something you put down the loo till Gordon told me it was some kind of savoury jelly,' she said. And the pre-show catering training that the group had done in west London before the show proper had begun had terrified her even more. 'I was so worried about how little I knew that I headed straight for my favourite pub, the Castle, near my home in Surrey, and worked as a kitchen slave for a weekend. That meant that on arrival in Gordon's domain I knew what to expect: fiendish hard work and intense pressure, especially during "service", when customers are waiting.'

What Edwina thought she had also learned was a way to deal with the legendary Ramsay temper. 'Christian, the chef at the Castle, had warned me that nothing said in a kitchen is ever personal and not to take it home. But I was ill-prepared for the endless foul-mouthed abuse – most of it counterproductive – that came our way in *Hell's Kitchen*. Sometimes I found it hilarious. I would wag my finger at Gordon when they weren't filming and tell him, "You wouldn't say that to your mother!" And "To someone my age, you are an infant not long out of your pram. How about acting like a grown-up?" That left him spluttering. If I didn't agree with something, I would also give Gordon a special look, one my mother used to do as well. It was a sort of "Who do you fucking think you are?" look without saying a single word. And for someone very verbal, such as Gordon, that was hard to deal with.'

Of course, long looks were not the only cross Gordon had to bear when it came to Edwina. Her souffles, and the drama that always accompanied whether they rose or fell, became another abiding moment of the show. As did the rows over her signature dish – the infamously greasy guinea-fowl confit. And the amount of salt in her risottos. Mix in all the other workers' various idiosyncrasies and it was easy to see the kitchen as a madhouse. Jennifer was triggering threatening letters from health and safety officers who said the restaurant would be closed down if she didn't stop wiping her nose on her tea towel, Matt was endlessly emotional, James was endlessly tearful, while Al seemed endlessly frustrated. 'The official nurses were on duty only intermittently, but a psychiatrist was available at all times,' confirmed Edwina when the madhouse comparison was put to her.

Fortunately for the former politician, the public seemed to prefer her histrionics to the more muted charms of Abi Titmuss. Gordon's 'hot totty' was the loser when she and Edwina went head to head in a public vote – much to Gordon's disgust. 'Edwina is like your old granny who just won't fucking die. This is a fucking disgrace,' Gordon moaned, head in hands after the announcement was made and he prepared to say goodbye to the Television X presenter.

However, losing Edwina at this stage would have meant missing out on what became one of the most famous quotes of the year. Having variously called Edwina 'poisonous', 'diseased' and 'a pathetic bitch', Gordon really let rip in a massive row when he focused on her shock affair with John Major. 'One minute you are shagging the Prime Minister and now you are trying to shag me from behind,' he roared – in a clip that would compete against his own 'Scallop-gate' throwing-up incident from *Ramsay's Kitchen Nightmares* in the battle for Best Factual Entertainment Moment of 2004. (In the event, neither Ramsay moment won: Jennie Bond got the award for her time lying underground in a rat-filled coffin in *I'm A Celebrity … Get Me Out Of Here!*)

Back in the Brick Lane kitchen, things were proceeding

just as staff at the group's original training centre had predicted. The staff at Ealing, Hammersmith and West London College had distilled the show's structure into an eight-step recipe. 'Step One: Take one no-nonsense chef with a reputation for straight-talking. Step Two: Add ten celebrities with barely an ounce of cooking expertise between them. Step Three: After a short amount of intensive training, place them all in the kitchens of London's newest and most exclusive restaurant. Step Four: Add to the mix a generous handful of celebrity diners and a sharp, critical viewing public to judge them. Step Five: Leave them all to simmer, removing any unwanted celebrities. Step Six: Turn up the heat on the remaining wannabe chefs, slowly evaporating more from the mix. Step Seven: Raise the temperature to the maximum and stand back as the remaining few come to the boil. Step Eight: Allow the public's taste to decide who should be the UK's newest celebrity chef.' After the attack on Edwina and Abi's surprising eviction, it looked as if everyone was well on their way to Step Seven.

But, as it turned out, it wasn't to be the hopeful celebrity chefs who were next to feel the heat. That weekend, the Sunday newspapers had a massive and potentially career-destroying shock up their sleeves for Gordon himself. They had just dug up an extraordinarily embarrassing incident from his past. And they were going to splash full details of it all over their pages.

'Gordon Ramsay, a drunken night out and gross indecency with two male chefs' was the shock *Mail on Sunday* headline that broke the story in the middle weekend of *Hell's Kitchen*. 'Celebrity chef Gordon Ramsay was cautioned for gross indecency after an incident with two other men in the lavatory of a London tube station. The married father of four, currently starring in ITV's hit reality show *Hell's Kitchen*, was arrested along with two other chefs after they were caught by the station manager,' the story began.

With papers such as the *Sunday Mirror* running the story under headlines like 'Flasher Gordon', it all seemed to resemble the 'lewd behaviour' that caused George Michael to be arrested in a public toilet in Los Angeles back in 1998. But Gordon's spokeswoman, Jo Barnes, was quick to play down all aspects of her client's brief brush with the law – which she said had been completely misinterpreted and had taken place more than a decade earlier.

'This incident took place in the early hours after a night of drinking and celebrating with friends which culminated in the three of them drunkenly horsing around in the loos of Green Park tube station. The station master, disturbed by the commotion, got the wrong end of the stick and notified the police, who arrested Gordon and the others upon leaving the loos. They were taken to West End Central Police Station where they received a caution.'

It had all happened back in March 1993 when Gordon had been learning his trade in Paris and had been back in London visiting friends. 'There was no court appearance involved. This was a complete boys' lark and there was nothing sexual involved,' continued Jo. 'This was a bunch of 20-something blokes, very, very drunk, messing around. As I understand it, they were in advanced stages of drunkenness and one of them was having a pee in the sink. The other one was running around with his trousers around his ankles and Gordon was actually just at a urinal with his head slumped against the wall. I think he was sick at one stage.'

Gordon himself did not discuss the incident either at the time or when news of it made the headlines in 2004. And he has never spoken of it since. Asked if he was embarrassed by the revelations, his spokeswoman said, 'You look back on yourself in your early twenties and you cringe a bit, don't you? I think there are lots of things we have done under the influence of alcohol that we are embarrassed about. Gordon does not really drink now, although not as a direct result of this incident. He is just a bit embarrassed about being a drunken idiot.' She also said that Gordon and his friends had accepted their cautions, as 'they wanted to get out of the police station as fast as possible'.

After a weekend reading revelations like those, coming back to work with television cameras rolling and millions watching was not for the faint-hearted. But come back Gordon did. The show had to go on and he hit the ground running as normal at the next morning's roll-call. In some ways, he actually had more reason for optimism as the restaurant's two-week stint drew to a close. The chefs were managing to produce quality food and diners were managing to get served, albeit after some long delays. An unhappy Al Murray was next to be evicted, donating nearly £23,000 to the disability charity Scope in the process. His departure left Edwina, Matt, James and Jennifer in contention for the top prize.

To Gordon's clear relief, Edwina lasted just one more day, then headed home to find friends had bought her a joke present of two Gordon Ramsay cookbooks, each with a knife sticking out of it. 'Thank God that is all over. I'm going to sleep for two days solid and eat nothing but Chinese and Indian meals and egg sandwiches,' she said. Having done so, she was ready to pass on her opinions of kitchen staff, her reasons for going on the show and, of course, of Gordon himself.

'I certainly developed a huge respect for anyone who works in a kitchen,' she said when the first subject was raised. 'Never again will I complain about a delay in a restaurant and I will always, always pay compliments for excellence.'

So why had she gone on a reality-television show? Partly to earn a decent amount of money, she was happy to admit, but also to get the chance to generate a large donation for her chosen charity, Marie Curie Cancer Care. And she said she was also keen to work with Gordon. 'It was a chance of a lifetime to work alongside him. He is one of Europe's great young chefs and a man passionately committed to good food. People would pay a fortune for that and there I was at the master's elbow,' she said. But, while it was no surprise that she hadn't enjoyed the experience, her overall analysis of his role in the show was sober stuff.

'Sadly, I have to say that I experienced a slide in my admiration for him,' she said. 'A man of his awesome stature should not be wasting his effort on a reality-television show like this. He didn't succeed in the challenge. Ten celebrities were not turned into top cooks, but were ground down by exhaustion and pain. Most would say he would have achieved a better result in a calmer atmosphere, but how interesting would that have been on our screens?'

In the Brick Lane restaurant, the celebrity diners – who now included Max Clifford, Jordan, Jerry Springer, Stephanie Beacham, Chris Eubank, Jade Goody, James Hewitt, Esther Rantzen and Sophie Anderton – may have taken exception to Edwina's view that Gordon hadn't produced any top cooks. The general feeling was that the standard of food being served was rising fast and was as good as you could expect in many, more established restaurants.

And the entertainment factor in the dining room remained equally high. The room itself was widely condemned as ugly – Steve Weids, manager of Harvey Nichols's wine department, memorably described the decor as 'Caravaggio meets porn' – but the personalities there easily made up for it. One of the ongoing sideshows to the events in the kitchen was Gordon's increasingly fraught relationship with Belgian head waiter Jean-Philippe Susilovic – immediately described as the Manuel to Gordon's Basil Fawlty. Jean-Philippe, or JP, had been drafted into *Hell's Kitchen* from Gordon's newly relocated Petrus and was well aware of his head chef's volatility. It was just as well. 'I think Gordon actually felt he couldn't shout at the celebrities as much as he wanted to,' he said after one particularly stressful evening in Brick Lane. 'So he shouts at me instead.' Always trying to soothe relations between Gordon in the kitchen and the group of angry celebrities in the dining room hungry for both food and publicity, Jean-Philippe was widely tipped as a possible candidate to replace Kofi Annan as head of the United

Nations. 'It would be an easier job,' he admitted after yet another expletive-strewn flare-up with his boss.

Matt Goss was the first of the final three to be voted off the show on the final night (all of them were from the original blue team). 'Gordon is a gentleman,' the singer said afterwards, despite having called him a wanker at the start of the show. 'I needed him to be tough, because that made me stronger and more confident.'

And then Angus Deayton came back into the kitchen as usual to read out the winner's name. James Dreyfus had missed out and the Celebrity Chef award went to Jennifer Ellison. 'I can't believe it, it's been the hardest thing I have ever done. I didn't know how to boil an egg before this show,' she admitted – just as Gordon offered her a job at Claridge's. 'She was a revelation, a complete surprise, the best chef in the house,' he said, praise immediately backed up by Mark Sargeant. 'Jen was a real natural; she had a clear head, a great memory and a bit of finesse about her. She could go on to any section and pretty much do it. She had common sense and she was able to follow instructions and keep it together when things went wrong,' he said, before offering her a job himself.

With the end-of-show party still in full swing, Gordon and Tana were driven back over the Thames to their home in Wandsworth. The experiment, the adventure, was over. In theory, *Hell's Kitchen* had taken just three weeks of Gordon's time: one for the initial training, two for filming. But when all the planning meetings, promotions and rehearsals had been taken into account it felt at times like three years. So had it been worth it?

As far as the ratings were concerned, the news was good.

The mid-series meltdown had been reversed and ITV said it had ended up over the moon about the audience share the show had delivered. Perhaps more importantly for Gordon, his staff told him that bookings hadn't slumped at any of his restaurants. Diners had not been put off by the thought that he was on television rather than in his kitchens, and were not now boycotting him in protest at his language or his treatment of his chefs. And while several high-profile rival chefs had spoken out against the show early on, the feeling among his peers seemed to be that it was a storm in a measuring cup. The Ramsay brand hadn't been damaged by the show. It looked like it was going to be strengthened by it, as Gordon had calculated all along.

On their return into his real kitchens, Gordon and his other chefs all felt invigorated as well. 'It's nice that people now know what an onion is when you tell them to go and get one,' said Angela Hartnett when asked how it felt to be back at the Connaught. 'And it's nice that they know how to peel it as well,' added Mark Sargeant, safely back at Claridge's.

For Gordon, it was just a relief to be back working among ordinary people. He says that after *Hell's Kitchen* he frequently found himself thinking along the same lines as Simon Cowell, that other equally honest television Mr Nasty. 'In my job I get up, go to work and get on with it, but the people in *Hell's Kitchen* didn't seem to be able to do that,' Gordon explained. 'The problem is really simply about truth – it is the truth to be told when you are crap at something, but these days most people just can't cope with that. I have never known people with such a huge amount of emotional baggage and I have never dealt with so much shit in my life.'

Unfortunately for him, Gordon was not going to be allowed to slip back into the relative obscurity of his hotel and restaurant kitchens for long. The bosses at ITV made a snap decision that they wanted a second series of *Hell's Kitchen* within a year. And they were so keen to have Gordon back at the helm that they were prepared to offer him £1 million for the privilege. That worked out as roughly £3,500 an hour of screen time, and would have catapulted Gordon from nowhere to the very top of the television earnings tree, well ahead of the hourly rates being paid to established stars such as Ant and Dec, Anne Robinson, Chris Tarrant and even Simon Cowell.

Even more tempting was the fact that there seemed to be no shortage of big-name stars who said they would run to be in his kitchen – some of them quite literally. Olympic gold medallist Dame Kelly Holmes was a prime example. 'Everyone is asking me what I am going to do next and one thing I would love to do is appear on *Hell's Kitchen*,' she said after watching the show. 'I can identify with Gordon because he wants perfection and that's what I have always been striving for all my professional life. He knows what it takes to reach the top, to be really good, and I can see he wants to pass that on to other people. So I wouldn't at all mind him shouting and swearing at me. My only worry would be that I might let him down.'

Gordon, however, was suddenly worried that he might have let himself down by taking part in the first series of *Hell's Kitchen*, let alone by agreeing to a second. The man who had said he wanted the words 'I am not a television chef' carved on his gravestone had finally finished reading some of the cuttings about the first show. One of them in particular stood out – the one in which the *Guardian* called him 'a celebrity chef turned gameshow host'. To a man as proud of his professionalism as Gordon, the description was horrific. But he had to admit that it rang ever so slightly true.

After building a career around winning Michelin stars, he realised he felt increasingly uncomfortable being put head to head alongside the likes of *Big Brother*'s Nadia when internet bank Smile put together its poll to find the 'celebrity of the year'. This wasn't exactly what he had been aiming for when he had left Ibrox and resolved to carve out a new career at the very top of the restaurant business. The man who had spent so long wishing his father was alive to see his triumphs suddenly felt very glad that he wasn't.

Gordon and Tana talked long and hard about the future in the first few weeks after the *Hell's Kitchen* set had been dismantled. They had a lot of cash in the bank – Gordon had collected an estimated £600,000 as star and co-creator of the original ITV show – so they knew money didn't have to be the driving force in their decisions. What mattered more, Gordon decided, was his long-term credibility. And if that meant a choice between *Hell's Kitchen* on ITV and *Ramsay's Kitchen Nightmares* on Channel 4, he would pick the latter every time. For all the hype, he still saw it as a constructive, even educational, show. As well as entertaining viewers, he reckoned, it was a way of putting something back into the restaurant industry and, hopefully, raising standards across the country. It was for that, rather than for hosting a 'gameshow', that he wanted to be known.

So Gordon called up the ITV bosses and gave them his answer. If they wanted to do a second series of *Hell's Kitchen*, they would have to find someone else to host it. He was going to keep his head down for a while and focus on his restaurants. He was also going to spend a bit more time at home with his children. Because the balance of power in the Ramsay household was changing. After so many years in her husband's shadow, it was Tana's turn to grab some of the limelight.

FIFTEEN
HAPPY FAMILIES

By the autumn of 2004, the Ramsay marriage was famous as one of the most enduring, if unorthodox, unions in show business. The pair certainly made a striking couple on their rare nights out in public together: Gordon with his broad shoulders, blond-streaked hair and sharp blue eyes, Tana petite and pretty with her flawless skin and big Julia Roberts smile. Always holding hands, constantly touching, they were clearly in love; even their clothes tended to complement each other – both in denim jackets for a quick meal at the Ivy, or in sparkling black shirts for a television awards show. And, as far as Gordon was concerned, the secret of their success could be explained in a single word: space.

'We get on like a house on fire, always have, but I dread to think what the relationship would be like if I was there seven nights a week. We would probably be divorced,' he admits.

For her part, Tana picks a different five-letter word to explain how their marriage has survived. Her word is 'trust'. 'Spending long periods apart, it's important that we trust one another,' she said. 'We speak up to ten times a day by phone. And when people ask, "How do you manage being on your own five nights a week?" I say, "Can you imagine having to think what to cook every night?" What we have may not work for everyone but it works very well for us.'

And behind all the chauvinistic comments and joking one-liners, Gordon is more romantic and more of a family man than he lets on. For many years, he closed his flagship restaurants at weekends purely to spend more time with his wife and family, for example – a decision industry analysts say cost him around £500,000 a year in lost revenue. Weekends had been important to the couple before they had children and they became essential as their family grew. 'From Monday to Friday, ours is a telephone relationship, so the weekends are catch-up time and the highlight of the week,' says Gordon. 'And when it comes to the kids I appreciate that, compared to some, we don't have a lot of time together, but I do make sure it is quality time. I'd rather be a dad fantastically twice a week than methodically five times a week.'

After getting home on Saturday morning at around 2am after his kitchens close, this 'fantastic dad' time tends to begin a lot sooner than he would like. 'If I'm lucky it will be 6.15 when the kids wake me. If I'm not, it may be 5.45. They'll prise open my eyelids, put their fingers in my ears, do whatever it takes to get me out of bed.' As befits a family headed by a chef, food can play a big part in any weekend's activities. The six-strong Ramsay clan can often be found wandering around farmers' markets in Pimlico, Borough or Chelsea on Saturday mornings, before having soup, salad or a sandwich for lunch. Or at least soups, salads and sandwiches are the theory. In reality, Gordon admits that healthy eating can be thwarted because just yards from the family's front door is a Pizza Express – and Britain's most Michelin-starred chef says he finds himself in it far more often than he would like. 'The kids love it, though Tana and I always say that the best thing to do before we take them there is to have a nice lunch ourselves first.'

Anything energetic for the kids is normally next on Gordon's agenda 'in a bid to get them all tired out', he says. But he accepts that he can sometimes drive Tana mad in the process. When he took three-year-old Jack out shopping for a new tracksuit one Saturday, the pair were gone so long that Tana finally rang Gordon's mobile to check that they hadn't got lost. 'Did you get the tracksuit?' she asked, when he reassured her that everything was fine and that they were on their way back home.

'No, I forgot,' he replied. 'But we did buy a rabbit.'

Father and son also share some secrets that might make Tana equally annoyed. Once a week, Gordon tries to take each of his children for lunch at a traditional cafe in Chelsea, for example. When it is Jack's turn, he always gets a Coke, though the pair tell Tana that he sticks to apple juice. 'We have a deal, we don't rat on each other, so he becomes my best mate, which is very important to me,' Gordon says.

At weekends, it is only after the kids' Saturday dinner, bath and story time that Gordon and Tana get to catch up with each other and with their friends – and Gordon is typically ungallant when it comes to describing what might be on offer if the Ramsays are hosting a party. He steers clear of the catering on his night off, and doesn't throw in many compliments about what Tana makes in his place. 'People might be anticipating the most amazing chicken fricassee with wild mushrooms and fresh tagliatelli, when what Tana will emerge with is a cottage pie – or Nigella's green Thai curry. Anyone expecting five-star treatment from me when they come round is certainly in for a disappointment. We certainly don't hold lavish dinner parties – too much like a busman's holiday.' Gordon may have his state-of-the-art £500,000 super-kitchen at home but it continues to be reserved solely for pleasure and for testing out new recipes. 'I mean it when I say I'm thinking about keeping the door locked at other times,' he says.

Tana, however, has suggested that the real reason for his uncharacteristic shyness about the kitchen could be that he doesn't actually know how to use a lot of the kit he had put in it. 'I can only serve you instant coffee,' she told *Metro* reporter Lisa Grainger when she came round to the house to interview her. 'Gordon has had an all-singing, all-dancing coffee machine installed but we are both so useless at technology that we haven't figured out how to use it. Give Gordon a sieve or a whisk and he's fine. But phones, videos, TVs, anything with buttons – forget it. When he sent me his first-ever romantic text message last week, I was so shocked that he had figured out how to do it that I had to phone him straight back to check it was really him.'

And having heard Gordon belittle the cottage pies and

green curries she cooks for their parties, Tana is also ready to fight back with a story of her own. 'At a dinner party in our old flat, Gordon got so carried away with his cooking that he set off all the home's smoke alarms. The children woke up and were screaming, the place was in chaos and it was pretty much the worst party we ever had,' she says.

On weekdays, the Ramsays continue to muddle through in their loving, idiosyncratic way. Amazingly, Gordon claims not to carry a key to his house. 'Every night he rings the bell whatever time it is. We make a cup of tea, take it to bed and catch up on the day's events,' says Tana of a routine many other wives would find intolerable. But late-night chats have always been the cornerstone of their relationship, right from the days when they would sit by the river outside Le Pont de la Tour or in Banbury after their restaurant shifts had ended, a time that they say now feels like several lifetimes ago. It is in the more recent late-night chats that they talk about the kids, their family and friends and the things they want to do. And in 2004 it was when Tana finally decided to go ahead with her new business venture.

'I fell in love with India about two years ago on a holiday,' she says. 'As a country it is quite mad but it works, and when I looked around at the things you can buy in the shops there I realised so much of their stuff would be suitable for homes over here as well.' The more Tana thought and talked about it the more she was convinced there was a business opportunity in importing and selling Indian goods. But could she really pull it off? For months, it became a big late-night topic of conversation with Gordon – and his view of her capabilities could be summed up in one short sentence. 'If you can manage four kids, you can do this,' he concluded just before she went ahead with her plan.

The business was set up in partnership with her brother, Adam, and Gordon was able to offer a simple suggestion when they started looking for premises. The building next to his new Boxwood Cafe had been up for rent ever since the superbly named Minema Cinema had closed a couple of years earlier. Tana and Adam took a look and realised it was perfect. By picking a location so close to one of Gordon's restaurants, Tana was also emphasising just how close her husband had become to her family. Many was the time that she and her brother were in the shop, at 41–5 Knightsbridge, while Gordon was less than a stone's throw away at the Boxwood Cafe with her father, Chris, finance director of Gordon Ramsay Holdings. And Gordon's loyalty to his extended family was complete. When Chris hit the headlines after being fined for breaking company law with his former firm, Kestrel Mould and Tooling Inc, his son-in-law refused to say a single word against him and said his position at Gordon Ramsay Holdings was entirely secure.

Fitting out the new shop, to be called the Red Fort, took longer than Tana and Adam had expected. They wanted it filled with Indian treasures, including every type of furniture from beds and benches to tables and temple doors. They wanted cushions, rugs, saris, bedspreads, jewellery, candles, spice boxes – the list went on and on. They also wanted the connections and contacts in place so that they could source any other goods that clients might require, including architectural features and stonework.

And, as the ever-growing stock list proved, they were thinking big from the very start. This was no vanity project for a rich wife, Tana said. It wasn't just a small local shop that could be managed on housekeeping money. The Red Fort was taking up several thousand feet of prime West End space and the stock and fitting out had cost £700,000. It had to make some real money from the moment it opened, so the pressure was on.

'This is your night, enjoy it.'

Gordon squeezed Tana's hand as they walked into the shop for its opening-night party. The event signalled the start of a new chapter in their lives together. For the first time they had hired a nanny to help out on the three days a week that Tana planned to work full-time, the days Megan was at school and the twins at a local nursery. And a few months later, when their new lives had bedded down, everyone was happy with the way it was working out.

'I've been the girlfriend, the wife, the mother, now it is about me again,' said Tana when she was asked how she felt. 'It's also like stepping out of Gordon's shadow. I don't need to go out and work but I don't want to live on the back of Gordon. I want to do my own thing, to have a life of my own and to find a niche beyond saying that dinner's ready and on the table at eight. The return to work has actually fitted well into our lives. Being at home with the children in the early years was a very important stage for them and I wanted to make sure that they had the best start in life. I was there for all the important moments, from the first words to the first steps. But the time came when it was right for me to go back to work. I love the buzz that my life has now. There is never a spare moment. Gordon has always thrived on that and I suppose it has inspired me too. We both sit down exhausted at the end of the day but we know that, although things have been manic, they have also gone right.'

The couple's late-night chats had also been given a new lease of life by Tana's new venture. 'Rather than: "Well, darling, I was washing up today and found this fabulous new brand of rubber gloves!" I can tell him about our achievements at work and ask his advice. We can have a proper conversation again,' she says. The kids were also thriving under the new regime – though something they told their mother one day showed that the foursome still had a lot to learn about their father. 'I am usually the one who disciplines the kids if they are being naughty,' says Tana. 'And after one telling-off they said, "Well, I'm going to cuddle Daddy now because he doesn't get cross." And off they all went to him.' Clearly, Megan, Jack, Holly and Matilda had not been allowed to watch *Ramsay's Kitchen Nightmares*.

When the children are in bed, Tana and Gordon say, they are not different from any other set of parents. 'Like any couple with young children, we argue, of course we do,' says Tana. 'I actually think that's important. It might be when he leaves his clothes on the floor thinking that the laundry fairy will come along and pick them up, or when he walks through the house in muddy trainers, not thinking that I'll have to clear up after him. But we both speak our minds, so problems don't get a chance to brew.

'Gordon can be fiery at work because he's a perfectionist and passionate about his job, so he takes it badly when things go wrong. But he doesn't shout and swear all the time at home, so I don't tend to see that side of him. The time when he is most relaxed is lying on the floor with the kids crawling all over him, just being Daddy. When the children were babies, they terrified him. He thought they were so tiny and helpless. But he's great with them now. Playing with them is how he relaxes.'

As the children got older, he also started, almost subconsciously, to take them into account when making business decisions at work. Would he ever serve ostrich and kangaroo meat in his restaurants? he was once asked by a catering student. 'No,' he said. 'Because what are you meant to say to your kids when you take them to the zoo and they see all those animals running around? How are you going to explain that?'

Both Gordon and Tana also think long and hard about their children when they plan their very rare, very short holidays – because neither wants to spoil them. 'My childhood holidays were spent in Blackpool, Scarborough, Bognor Regis and Loch Lomond and I didn't get on a plane till I was 21, so doing so meant a lot to me. I don't want the kids to be blase about all those things,' says Gordon. So, while they have multi-millionaire parents, the Ramsay children still spent one of their first family holidays at Butlins in Minehead with their grandmother to ensure they keep their feet firmly on the ground. Other more upmarket family treats managed to leave Gordon cold. 'Bores the crap out of me,' he told BA's in-flight magazine *High Life* about trips to Disney World.

What interested him a lot more were the secret 'boyfriend and girlfriend holidays' that he and Tana take once a year. Saying the breaks are vital escape valves that help keep them both sane, the couple fly off for just a few days alone together while Tana's parents and Gordon's mum take turns to look after the children. 'It's like dating again,' says Tana, who tries to recreate the holiday mood throughout the rest of the year as well. 'It's important to allocate time just for you as a couple. So, on Sunday nights, for example, when the children are in bed, we hire a babysitter and either go to the cinema or Gordon cooks dinner for me. I find it healthy that we are not in each other's pockets all the time. Maybe that's why we are still so passionate about each other.'

And, according to Gordon, 'passionate' is exactly the right word to use. Over the years, he has missed few opportunities to discuss the couple's sex life, his own prowess between the sheets or sex in general. 'Food is a very sensual thing. When you have a turbot in front of you, you can't help but think along the lines of making a woman feel happy in ways that she wouldn't believe,' he said, bizarrely, at one point. 'There's something strangely sensual about making ravioli,' he said at another, before admitting, 'Cooking is like having the most massive hard-on plus Viagra sprinkled on top of it and it's still there 12 hours later.' And then there was the time in *Hell's Kitchen* when he said he wanted the celebrities to take a stick of salsify or an artichoke to bed. 'You will be surprised what you learn from it,' he said, slightly worryingly, without going into any more details.

But absolutely nothing goes unsaid or is left to the imagination when Gordon starts discussing his and Tana's own personal lives. 'I ring Tana up from the restaurant and ask, "Are you up for it?" Then, in the middle of the chat, there will be a fuck-up in the kitchen, I'll get angry with one of the staff and Tana will go, "Ooh, can you come home right now, that sounds amazing!" So, if I can, I head right off.' Gordon also claimed that Tana likes him to keep his chef's outfit on while they make love – something she has never publicly confirmed.

What Tana has found is that, when your husband talks to journalists about your sex life at the drop of a chef's hat, you then get all the same questions when you give interviews yourself. And, while she is far more discreet than Gordon, Tana does back up a lot of his claims. 'Sometimes, if we're at a party, he will look across the room and wink and I just think, Hello! Yes, the chemistry is still there and we do have a very passionate sex life,' she says when questioned directly on the subject. 'But I'd really rather keep it to myself. I say to Gordon, "You do realise that my parents might be reading this?" I think he is finally getting the message that I feel a little bit embarrassed and I'm not comfortable with him bragging about it all.'

What neither Gordon nor Tana brags about is the work they both do for charities. For example, they regularly make quiet visits to the shelter for battered wives where Gordon's mother had sought shelter from her husband when Gordon was living in London. 'They never make any fuss but they always bring down some of the children's old clothes and toys,' says Helen. And in London, Gordon's old clothes and size-12 shoes are taken to a centre for the homeless and people with alcohol problems.

In a more high-profile manner, Gordon has managed to raise well over £100,000 for a host of different charities over the years through his marathon running. A regular at the London Marathon (where he was once humiliated to learn that television gardener Charlie Dimmock had beaten him by eight minutes), he has picked causes ranging from the women's refuge and the Food Chain, which offers meals to people with HIV, to the premature-birth charity Tommy's and Sport Relief, which helps youngsters in inner cities and other areas channel their energies into sport rather than crime or drugs.

Running marathons has always been a favourite activity for Gordon, and one he shares with Tana. It seems a strange choice because the training takes up so much time and time is the one thing Gordon has very little of. But it is obvious when you consider his background as the utterly driven, fiercely competitive son of a sports-centre manager. Fitness was clearly vital for Gordon as a professional footballer. And when he became a chef his nightly runs brought two other key benefits. First, they allowed him to clear his head and freshen up after long hours in the hot, humid, noisy and angry kitchen environment. Second, and very simply, they offered him a convenient and cheap way of getting home after a late-night shift when public transport was thin on the ground and he was surviving on rock-bottom wages.

'I would run down along the Thames totally alone, watching the patterns on the water from the embankment and from the bridges. It's so quiet when there's not much traffic, a magical, beautiful experience,' he says. 'Running gives me fresh air, freedom and quiet time to myself. It's the best way of de-stressing.' Running also helped him woo Tana in the early days of their relationship. With next to no spare time, they turned Sunday-morning jogs into dates, pretty much running, talking and falling in love all at the same time, according to Gordon.

The man who has spent a lifetime testing, proving and pushing himself was never going to be content just jogging at the weekend, or running home from work in the week, however. He started entering races when he was still working with Michel Roux at Le Gavroche, not knowing that years later he and his mentor would both be running in the same London Marathon. (To his embarrassment, despite a massive media interest in the rivalry between the two chefs, Gordon's finishing time of three hours eighteen minutes would put him behind both Michel and fellow runner Tana in the cold and rainy 2004 event.)

Over the years, Gordon has kept running and competing in order to fight off the downside of kitchen life. 'Chefs don't sit and eat proper meals during the day – we graze – and that's a bad way to live and eat. By running, I am able to enjoy eating without putting too much weight on.' He wasn't alone. Over the years, he has persuaded scores of his colleagues to join him out on the road. In the seven most serious months of pre-London Marathon training, they tend to run two nights a week, normally Tuesdays and Thursdays, as well as doing half-marathons on Sundays. On the big day, Gordon has sometimes had at the starting line with him up to a dozen staff members, from wine waiters to dish washers, plus his equally dedicated father-in-law.

Tana's dad often arrives at the Ramsays' front door in his running kit early on a Sunday morning to see if either his daughter or son-in-law is ready for a pre-breakfast race. And, unable to compete with his own father, Gordon is almost always prepared to compete with Tana's. That could go some way to explain why, having realised he is unlikely to match the 50-plus marathons Chris has finished, Gordon decided to try to beat the older man at a slightly different game. In 2001, he decided to take up double marathons, including the ferociously testing 'Comrades' challenge that takes place every year in South Africa. 'It is 59 miles and the terrain is as tough as the distance,' says Gordon. 'You need to give it everything you have from the start because, if you don't finish the first marathon in less than a certain amount of time, you are pulled from the competition.' In his first attempt, Gordon made the cut and crossed the finishing line in ten and a half hours.

But, in 2004, he wasn't as successful and had to stop at the 30-mile point before being taken to hospital by helicopter suffering from leg injuries and exhaustion. So, with 40 just a couple of years away, was Gordon's body no longer up to the challenge? Not surprisingly, he was having none of it. As he became increasingly notorious for his expletive-strewn television appearances, he says, the problem was that, if he could train at all, he had to try to do so in disguise – even in the early hours of the morning. 'There always seems to be groups of builders in white vans yelling out: "Table Onze, you fucker!" if I'm not hidden away under a cap,' he says.

Heading to the 'big five' hills around Durban for the Comrades challenge wasn't the only trip Gordon made to Africa, however. The Comic Relief charity asked him to visit a village in Tanzania alongside Lenny Henry in December 2002. At first, pairing the two men seemed like great fun. In the 1900s, Lenny had famously created the character of Gareth Blackstock for his sitcom *Chef!* Gareth was described as 'The *enfant terrible* of culinary art, impossibly difficult to work for, anally fastidious about his creations and possessing a volcanic temper and savage tongue.' It is like looking in the mirror, the pair had joked when they had first met shortly after the show had aired. But they both found very little to laugh about when they got together again for the Comic Relief fundraiser.

The idea behind the trip was for Gordon to use local ingredients and cook as good and nutritious a meal as he could for around a hundred street children – but he and Lenny had to do so without a kitchen, without running water and without outside help. What they saw in Africa shocked them from the moment their plane landed. 'It was Christmas in London and eight and a half hours later you are in the bleakest place in the world,' said Gordon. 'We saw kids of three or four sleeping in the gutters by a sewage pipe with no caring adults anywhere around to look after them. It was awful, just awful,' said Lenny.

Determined to hide their feelings, the pair threw themselves into the job in hand, chopping wood, building fires, putting together the huge pot of flour, oats and water to make ugali, the street kids' favourite food, then washing everything up to stress the importance of basic hygiene.

The men said none of it was easy, either mentally or physically. 'I know it probably sounds a bit wet, but I cried for four nights on the trot,' Gordon said afterwards. 'I was close to tears, big time, during the day, but I was determined not to cry in front of the kids. So you needed to break down in the evening, after you'd finished work, to get it off your chest so that you could get through the next day. To make matters worse, it was not just the poverty that was so terrible. The kids sniff glue to comatose themselves when darkness falls, because that's when they get attacked and abused. Guys terrorising youngsters, waiting to pounce. Come midnight, it's evil. Night-time in Arusha is like Baghdad in the middle of war.'

As is so often the case in such terrible situations, it was the individual stories that hit home the hardest. 'I met a young guy called Alex who had been sexually abused by his grandfather. His dad had got another woman and his mum had run away, so he was on his own. We just clicked when he grabbed my hand, tried to speak in broken English. He was dying for his mum – he described her as his best mate – and he hadn't seen her in seven years. I know how important my mum is to me. But I made a big mistake. I gave him some money to buy shoes and he was beaten up for it.' Later, when serving food to the villagers, Gordon gave Alex some seconds – and nearly caused a riot. Throughout the short trip, Gordon says he was haunted by the contrast between life in rural Tanzania and life back in London.

'I had come from Claridge's just before Christmas, where it was all Champagne and caviar. Yet, when we cooked for these kids, it was the first time many of them had eaten properly in so long. The culture shock was extraordinary and, while I don't regret anything I have ever done in my life, I wish I had experienced something like this a little earlier on. It has taught me so much and given me so much new perspective.'

Feeling physically sick, unable to eat surrounded by such poverty and suffering, and unable to forget what he had seen once he was back in London, Gordon says he ultimately lost two and half stone as a direct result of the experience. When Alex Ferguson came into his restaurant one day shortly afterwards, he said the chef looked 'as rough as a gypsy's dog'. And, as a consequence of it all, Gordon changed the way his family ate at home as well.

'Little Alex is a legend in our house now. I told the kids all about him and we all watched the videos from Africa so they know how fortunate they are. They know they're lucky to have food. Megan had a bowl of Honey Nut Loops but she only ate half of them and I got upset. Waste now makes me sick, knowing how appreciated that would be over there. So Tana and I decided that we'll give the kids half portions. If they want more, they'll ask.' That Christmas, having seen and heard about Alex and the other children in Africa, the Ramsay children were also asked to give up some of their own toys for charity before being given their presents. Gordon says he nearly cried again when none of them hesitated for as much as a second before doing so.

'Come on, Doodles.' More than three years after his African experience, Gordon swings a giggling Megan on to his shoulders before taking her to the local public pool for a Sunday-morning swim. Sundays are her morning – after Gordon takes Jack to his tiny tots' football training on a Saturday. And, whatever Megan, Jack, Holly and Matilda do, Gordon tries always to remember to praise and support them.

'What happened between me and my dad will never happen between me and my children,' he says, his voice uncharacteristically quiet, his intention clear. 'I hope to be the one they will remember as having always been there to pick up the pieces for them. Not as one who said "I told you so" when things when wrong. Whatever they choose to do in life I will be behind them one hundred per cent. All I want for them is that they'll be happy, doing whatever it is that they themselves choose to do. Kicking a football. In a kitchen. Whatever.'

That said, Gordon's fatherly advice for his son, in particular, can still be typically blunt. 'I tell Jack if he doesn't eat spinach his widger won't grow' is just one nugget of Ramsay wisdom that leaves Tana rolling her eyes at tea-time.

'The Gordon Ramsay that strangers read about or see on their televisions is not the Gordon I see at home' is how Tana sums up their unconventional but successful domestic life. And she says her famously rude, insensitive and chauvinistic husband really does have a sensitive side. 'He tells me he loves me several times a day. And when one of the children says, "I love you, Daddy," he always has the same reply. "Not as much as I love you."'

SIXTEEN

MEETING MOMMA CHERRI

Several thousand delegates representing the cream of the country's restaurant trade were on the P&O cruise ship *Oriana* in 2005 when they were asked which famous chef they thought was the most positive role model for their industry.

'Jamie Oliver,' said six out of ten.

'Gordon Ramsay,' said one in ten.

'Well, that's a load of bollocks,' said Gordon himself, who was one of the keynote speakers on the cruise and left the boat shortly after the survey results had been announced. More than a decade after starting his catering career, Gordon was as ready to speak his mind as ever.

His problem, however, was persuading people that his straight talking always came from the heart. 'With *Hell's Kitchen* I was in danger of becoming a caricature of myself,' he realised after watching the tapes and reading the press coverage. All the onscreen anger and the frustrations had been genuine, but he detected a whiff of Anne Robinson in some of his putdowns and people were asking if he was acting for the cameras rather than really caring about the quality of the food. His lifelong fear of losing credibility resurfaced – and this turned out to be one of the major reasons why he turned down ITV's £1-million offer to host a second series of the show.

Giving up such a huge pay cheque was made ever so slightly easier by the fact that an even bigger rival offer was waiting in the wings, however. Channel 4 had stumped up a reported £1.2-million deal to take in more *Ramsay's Kitchen Nightmares* and any other shows the chef wanted to make. 'It let me out of the straitjacket,' he said when asked why he accepted it. He also said he loved the pure challenge of *Kitchen Nightmares*: heading out on the road, finding out how close the chosen restaurants might be to disaster and working out if they could be saved. Fortunately for everyone, the next set of restaurants the producers had found for him turned out to be crackers.

'He's back, and he's as angry as ever,' screamed the posters as the second series of *Ramsay's Kitchen Nightmares* prepared to hit the screens in the summer of 2005. For once, the advertisers weren't exaggerating, and the first show of the series introduced viewers to a chef who would become almost as infamous as Tim, from Bonaparte's, a year earlier. 'The show casts Gordon, quite unmistakably, as Freddy from the *Nightmare on Elm Street* franchise,' wrote Pete Clark in the *Evening Standard* after watching a preview tape. 'Freddy, you may recall, invaded the dreams of impressionable young people in order to butcher them.

My understanding was that the Gordon Ramsay franchise was a kinder and more caring operation, but there were times last night when it seemed likely that Alex, a young and impressionable chef, was about to make history by being served to his customers, pan-fried in his own juices.'

Alex, it turned out, had big dreams, the main one being to produce 'modern Italian food in a modern style'. Unfortunately for his customers, this seemed to involve taking vegetables straight from the local Tesco to his microwave, using packet sauces and failing to fully defrost any of his puddings. 'This is about as authentic as a fucking Chinese takeaway' was Gordon's initial assessment of Alex's La Lanterna restaurant in Letchworth, Hertfordshire. And things soon got worse.

'It looks like two penises on a plate,' Gordon said when the 29-year-old chef put one of his favourite sausage dishes in front of him. He also found out that Alex's taste buds left a little bit to be desired. From his early twenties, Gordon had been obsessed by training his palate to recognise the best foods and the finest flavours. Alex, it is fair to say, had never really thought much about his palate. So, when Gordon conjured up a fantastic piece of television theatre and arranged a blind tasting test where the youngster had to pick the best between a Gordon Ramsay signature dish and a Pot Noodle, the result was never really in doubt. Alex said he much preferred the Pot Noodle.

He also refused to accept Gordon's criticisms of his food. 'I learned everything from a well-respected Italian chef,' he claimed, outraged that his Italian dishes weren't considered up to scratch. Not quite believing it, Gordon tracked the man down – and found him working as a taxi driver.

Maybe all this would have been just about acceptable to Gordon had Alex been more aware of his shortcomings. But, with the cameras rolling, he found out just how out of touch the youngster was – he had paid a fortune to attach the number plate A1 6HEF to his car, even though Gordon said he was a million miles from the A-list. It was the final straw and Gordon was ready to let rip with his early assessment of everything he had seen. 'The whole place is straight out of an eighties fake trattoria,' he said in despair. 'The food is fucking disgusting and this place is in such meltdown that he's even let the most basic standards of hygiene slip. It's a breeding ground for rats, mice and all kids of pests. The biggest one is Alex. He's been scurrying around in his own filth for far too long. And I've got a good mind to get that number plate off his car and stick it up his arse sideways.'

As usual, what he did instead was to coach and coerce Alex into raising his game. The pair started off with a massive cleaning job in the kitchen and a clear-out of the long, fussy menu that Alex could never hope to handle. All the staff – including the unlikely combination of Alex's best mate and his ex-girlfriend, who were in charge of the front of house – got shouted into shape. Amazingly, one of Gordon's chief rivals inadvertently stepped in to help. Gary Rhodes opened his chequebook when Alex agreed to sell his A1 6HEF number plate to help pay off the restaurant's ever-growing overdraft and provide some funds for a relaunch. But would it all work? As usual, one of the best parts of the programme came when Gordon returned six weeks later to see if the nightmare was over. And at La Lanterna it looked as if it was.

'This is exactly the kind of food Alex should have been serving all along,' said Gordon, stunned and happy when he returned to find the chef making fresh ravioli, spaghetti with meatballs and genuine Italian desserts.

Alex was smiling just as broadly. 'It has been an amazing experience. Where we were taking in £2,000 a week we have now doubled it and are beyond our break-even point. I hadn't seen the first series of *Kitchen Nightmares* when I signed up to take part but friends who knew the show said, "Are you mad? He'll slaughter you." But I am so glad I did it. Gordon's an amazing guy and he's helped me save my business.'

But not everyone was as happy. As part of the original turnaround of La Lanterna, Gordon had gone out into the street offering pizza to passers-by to try to show Alex how well they would respond to simpler, better Italian food. On camera, Gordon assured one vegetarian volunteer that the pizza on offer was meat-free – before admitting that the base was in fact covered in Parma ham. 'Good luck with the Vegemite,' he yelled after the pedestrian, triggering a massive wave of criticism. As fate would have it, the programme was aired in National Vegetarian Week and the Vegetarian Society was up in arms. Its top brass said they believed Gordon had broken European law by tricking the vegetarian into eating meat on camera and were desperate to trace the man. 'We'd like him to get in touch as there could be a test case under the European Convention on Human Rights,' said a spokesman.

While nothing ever came of the claim, it wasn't the first time Gordon had annoyed the Society's members. A couple of years earlier, he had joked about telling a table of vegetarians that the artichoke soup they were eating had been made with chicken stock rather than vegetable stock, even though it hadn't. He had also defined a bad day as 'one where 25 vegetarians turn up unannounced' at one of his restaurants and said people who don't eat meat are 'a real pain in the arse'.

Over the years, his views had mellowed enormously, however, and he had introduced vegetarian menus into all his restaurants, and says he loves coming up with new ideas for them. And, while analysts and anoraks totted up that Gordon still swore roughly once every 40 seconds in this second series of *Ramsay's Kitchen Nightmares*, he did seem to be making more friends than enemies. The biggest, brightest and most memorable of them turned out to be Charita Jones, the owner of Momma Cherri's Soul Food Shack, buried deep in the winding Lanes of Brighton.

'Y'all gotta come to me. Ain't no one like me in the country. You gotta come see me,' she had begged the show's producers when they were looking for restaurants in need of the Ramsay touch. But, when they agreed, she laid down her ground rules from the start. 'When Gordon came round, I told him, "Listen, I am a churchgoing woman. You'd better mind your language."'

Unfortunately, this wasn't going to be an easy request for Gordon to stick to. Because he soon found a lot to swear about.

For once, though, the problem wasn't with the food. Gordon sat down, read the menu, looked at the food, tasted it and loved it. 'He didn't look that impressed when he walked in the restaurant but I fixed him catfish goujons with pineapple salsa and a cornbread with vegetable I call hush puppies. Then he had meat jambalaya, baby back ribs with barbecue sauce, a sweetcorn and broad beans dish called succotash plus coleslaw and salad. His plate was just piled up. And when he handed me back his plate it had just four bones on it. I grabbed my camera and took a picture. I said, "Whether y'all do this film or not, Gordon Ramsay cleaned his plate in my restaurant!" He said, "I feel like I've been to my mother's," and I took that as a big compliment. Even if I had to close tomorrow, that did it for me.'

But Gordon did want to do the film with Charita. And he could tell she needed help if she wanted to stay open. She might well be serving the best soul food in Britain but her restaurant hadn't made a penny in profit in four years and, with her debts topping £65,000, the banks were closing in.

The key reason, Gordon said, was that she was too nice to her staff, paying most of them more than she paid herself and putting up with any number of unexplained absences and sudden departures. Too many of them, he said, were part-timers who showed part-time commitment. And none seemed to really know what they ought to be doing. 'I hate to ruin a good party but, if you want to run a good business, then the terms "laid-back" and "professional" don't mix,' said Gordon, foreshadowing Sir Alan Sugar in *The Apprentice*. 'The food is not the problem here. It's the way you are running everything. You are too much of a mother. You baby all your staff. You let them get away with murder.'

In one bit of classic television, he found out that Charita's chef was at home with childcare problems, leaving her to do all his work that day. Stopping Charita in her tracks as she tried to make excuses for her chef, Gordon and the film crew headed out to the chef's home with all the ingredients he should have been preparing. Off camera, they continued to talk through his problems, tried to find solutions – and got him to work on the food at the same time to take the pressure off his boss.

What Gordon also did was to persuade Charita to play to her own formidable strengths. He told her to leave the kitchen to the others and get out into the dining room and into the streets of Brighton to drum up business. An entire new menu was also created. It was simpler, cheaper and, with the new name 'Soul in a bowl', it was a whole lot easier to promote.

So, six weeks later, had it all worked? In the second half of a feel-good episode that matched Gordon's *Faking It* show with Ed Devlin of nearly four years earlier, it turned out that it had. Charita had managed to stick to most, if not all, of Gordon's instructions. And, while her debts would take years to clear, more customers were at last coming through her doors. On one memorable night, all 40 seats in the restaurant were full and people were being turned away – something that had never happened before.

'I was like a sponge, taking in what Gordon said and giving everything a try. He had my chefs sweating but it was just the push they needed. I thought all I had to do was cook food and put it on plates. Gordon taught me how to kick ass. He taught me I don't have to be so nice,' said Charita. And he was certainly the right man to teach that particular lesson.

The episode also served to silence the critics who said Gordon was playing to the cameras and only interested in humiliating and embarrassing the chefs and restaurant owners featured in it. Instead, he proved that he really could help turn ailing businesses around – with some brilliant entertainment thrown in. So, at the end of this episode, Charita and Gordon were incredibly close, with the ever-sassy Charita just about holding on to the upper hand.

'Will you adopt me?' Gordon asked the woman who over the years had fostered more than 30 kids and raised two of her own.

'Yes, I will,' she replied. 'But you've got to wash your mouth out first.'

Unfortunately, not everyone Gordon had met while filming *Ramsay's Kitchen Nightmares* over the years would stay in such good spirits. The bosses of D-Place in Chelmsford could be forgiven for a sense-of-humour failure: their 'global cuisine' restaurant had shut its doors even before Gordon returned to check on progress six weeks after giving them his survival strategy.

But one other restaurant had closed in even more acrimonious fashion. In Silsden, West Yorkshire, a 'For Sale' sign was hanging outside the premises of Bonaparte's – the first restaurant that Gordon had tackled in the previous series of the show a year earlier, where the world had been introduced to 21-year-old trainee chef Tim Gray. During and immediately after filming, the owner, Sue Ray, said she was pleasantly surprised by Gordon's manner. 'He is really a sheep in wolf's clothing. He does not pull any punches, but he's really charming and good fun, quite the opposite of how he normally appears on television. We had a bit of a laugh with him and he's actually a very pleasant guy.'

One year on, she had changed her mind completely and

said dicing with the kitchen devil had been a disaster from start to finish. 'They said they were here to help. They said the show would make the restaurant profitable but in the programme they just focused on the negative and made a laughing stock out of me. They certainly didn't say there were going to call the show *Kitchen Nightmares*, make a fool out of me and destroy my business. It was very cruel,' she said of Ramsay, the producers and the edited version of the show that had been broadcast about her.

Tim was equally unhappy. 'I think I came out of it worse than anyone and it wasn't all down to me. A friend called me afterwards and asked me how it felt to be the biggest twat in Britain?'

Unable to make the restaurant pay despite trying to introduce the changes Gordon had suggested, Sue had shut it down and was now struggling just to run a bar in the same building. When the second series of the show was about to be broadcast, she warned anyone else against taking part, telling the *Daily Mail* that the experience had ruined her life, left her with £500,000 of debts, the prospect of bankruptcy, deep depression and a desire only to move to live in a camper van in Spain. 'Gordon Ramsay was extremely negative and destructive with me. The programme crippled me and I am just waiting for the axe to fall from the bank. I have been on tablets for depression, we were getting hate mail, the programme had terrible repercussions. I currently have a flat above Bonaparte's but when the building is sold I am out of house and home. The bank will repossess it if it is not sold and even if it is I won't see a penny of the money because I owe so much. Ramsay has taken everything from me. I am thinking of going down to London and sleeping outside Claridge's to embarrass him.'

The producers advised her not to and the show's publicist, Julie Pickford, rejected Sue's claims that she had been stitched up. 'We invited people to apply to the show if they felt they could benefit from the wisdom Gordon could offer. There were big issues at Bonaparte's restaurant and they were discussed at the beginning of the programme when Sue told Gordon the reasons for inviting him in. She had full opportunity to have her say. Gordon's reputation precedes him. It's not as if people didn't know what to expect with him.'

Once bitten, twice shy, Sue was outraged when Gordon subsequently turned up to try to film a follow-up programme. 'How dare you? I thought. You cheeky bastard. You've done enough damage.' Gordon, however, remained convinced that, despite all the drawbacks, Bonaparte's could be turned into a success. 'I still believe Sue could make it work but she has to learn that to run a restaurant she first has to run a clean kitchen,' he said.

He believed she should also take on board that nowadays all publicity really can be good publicity. Charita Jones believed it, and so too did Neil Farrell, who had nearly come to blows with Gordon when the Glass House was featured a week after Bonaparte's in that first series. 'Halfway through the actual programme, we had 10,000 hits on our website and within a week of it ending we had 183,000 hits,' he said. 'That's when I thought, This isn't so bad. It's easy to swallow your pride when you see a positive effect on your business.'

While he had laid into Gordon's professionalism in the

first few days after his episode had been broadcast, Neil ultimately softened his views. In the end, he even had the story of the show written up on the back of the restaurant's menus to drum up even more publicity and interest. 'Overall we have gained more than we have lost and that is down to Ramsay giving me a kick up the butt,' he said. Neil was also ready with some secret advice for anyone following in his footsteps by taking part in the show. 'Out of the blue one night, I got a call from the owner of one of the restaurants being featured in the new series,' he says, though he won't reveal who it was. 'He was in floods of tears and Gordon had only been there for one day. He was crying, "How can I get rid of this terrible man?" All I could say was: "Don't let the bastard see you cry."' Neil also tried to persuade his caller that it was worth staying the course and listening to what Gordon had to say, however painful that might be.

The experts agreed that there were long-term advantages to getting Gordon's advice, and that there was more to the show than just good television. 'Gordon creates drama to identify with,' said Professor Kim James of the Cranfield School of Management. 'But the ultimate test of a leader is their legacy and Ramsay's greatest gift to the restaurants he turns around will be to leave them capable of good theatre when he is no longer the star.'

Gordon was also hoping that customers would do some of his work for him in other underperforming restaurants, though he despairs of the fact that British diners are strangely incapable of fighting for their rights. 'I don't think customers are tough enough. Food, on the whole, is getting miles better in this country. Shops and supermarkets have improved, we're moving forward as a nation. But we lack the confidence to question the standards in a restaurant. You're paying for it, though, so it's your right. If you go and buy a car, you make sure you get value for money, a three-year warranty, a service history, and you look at securing part-exchange three years down the line. You scrutinise everything. But going out to dinner, we just sit there like lambs to the slaughter and just accept what's given.'

Or do we? Some experts had credited Gordon with changing that as well, identifying a 'Ramsay effect' that was making us a more demanding nation. Advertising firm Publicis said we had seen how Gordon and the likes of Sharon Osbourne got results by being direct, and were following suit. 'We are following their examples, rejecting the stiff upper lip and becoming more volatile and more verbally and emotionally demonstrative,' said Paul Edwards. 'We're no longer so ashamed of making our views clear and we're getting angry in public more often.'

What Gordon was also doing, when the cameras had stopped rolling, was to try to change the lives of some of the talented and hopeful chefs that he met while filming his various programmes. Relatively experienced workers such as Spencer Ralph at the Walnut Tree and Andy Trowell at Moore Place in Esher, Surrey, were given some behind-the-scenes encouragement to help them develop their careers, while those at the very bottom of the catering pile were also offered a lift. Claire Porter, the 24-year-old part-time chef at the Glass House in Ambleside, was a prime example of the latter. Claire had never been to catering college, was running a bookshop as her day job and only ended up in the Glass House's kitchen after trying to earn some extra money by working evening shifts in the front of house. Gordon, however, said he knew she had potential from the start, and that she reminded him of Angela Hartnett, one of his most successful proteges, who was now heading up his restaurant at London's luxury Connaught Hotel. After long, private pep talks with Claire, Gordon persuaded her to consider catering as a full-time career. She left Cumbria for London, where he helped her get an interview and then a job on the Connaught's garnish section alongside Angela herself.

Another potential rising star had also been spotted at the Glass House: new recruit Ian Waddell. 'I can't believe you've only been cooking for three months. You're a fucking natural,' Gordon said after seeing the youngster at work. Equally inspired by Gordon's behind-the-scenes encouragement, Ian followed Claire down to London and was offered a job as demi chef de partie at Gordon's flagship restaurant at Claridge's – one of the most prestigious dining rooms in the capital. Unfortunately, Ian didn't last long in Gordon's long-hours culture. 'Ian had a natural gift and was definitely a great chef in the making and I am gutted he didn't last the course,' his former boss, Neil, said when he heard that the lad had left the Ramsay empire and gone off to work for an outside catering company in London's Canary Wharf instead. 'He came from a kitchen where things were a bit of a laugh,' Neil said, and 19-hour-days just repeating the same task in London turned out to be anything but.

Sadly, Claire was also finding things tougher than expected in London. She left the Connaught just after Ian left Claridge's. But Gordon said neither move would stop him offering similar opportunities to any other high-potential staff he spotted while filming future episodes of the show.

And the resignations could hardly take a new smile off Gordon's face anyway. For something far more important than a mere catering career was happening on the other side of the world. Having lost more than a decade of his life, his brother Ronnie was finally off drugs, out of rehab and in the pink.

The total turnaround had begun almost exactly a year earlier, when Ronnie and the Ramsay family had all appeared to be at their lowest point. 'I hope Ronnie finds happiness, but to preserve ourselves we've had to stop contact,' his heartbroken mother had said, as yet another tough-love battle began. 'It's so sad what has happened to him. He has had the best of help, but it hasn't made any difference.'

'Ronnie is on his own now,' Gordon had confirmed back in the summer of 2004, supporting his mother and accepting that he might never see his younger brother again. At that point, Ronnie, who had once weighed the same as fifteen-stone Gordon, was clocking in at little more than a sickly seven and a half stone. He was believed to be spending £100 a day feeding his drug habit. Gordon was convinced the phone call saying his brother had died, the one he had secretly dreaded for more than a decade, could come any day, and the whole family was braced for the worst.

But, as it turned out, no phone call came. Instead, Gordon received a mysterious letter from a stranger who had just come home from Bali. The writer, known only as Mark, was a reformed drug addict himself and he had first heard about Gordon and his brother Ronnie while working as a Red Cross volunteer after the bombing in Bali in 2002. One night, a chef on the island had been talking about the foul-mouthed Scottish chef with the troubled brother and on a whim Mark wrote to Gordon explaining how volunteer work had helped him kick his habit and build a new life. He suggested that Ronnie might benefit from something similar.

Gordon remembers sitting at home in Wandsworth talking about the letter with Tana. Was it a hoax? A joke? Too good to be true? And wasn't Ronnie finally past saving? The whole family had recently decided that there was no point in giving Ronnie one more chance and that they should now keep their distance and leave him to sink or swim. Should Gordon go back on his word and re-engage him? Gordon and Tana talked even later into the night than usual and they both read and reread the letter dozens of times, trying to decide what to do. The next day Gordon decided he would take action. His brother was always going to be worth one more try.

Gordon tracked down the letter writer, who had since come back to Britain. He rang him, met him, got to know him and then put a proposition to him. In short, he wanted Mark to be his brother's full-time buddy, 24 hours a day, seven days a week if necessary. Tell him your story, try to inspire and support him, Gordon asked. See if one day he can become like you. Mark agreed, but everyone knew things were going to be tough. Before the mentoring could even begin to work, Ronnie had to get clean one more time, so another gruelling period of rehab was on the cards. This was to be Ronnie's seventh major attempt at rehab, and experts say that in many cases the process gets harder every time it is faced again.

This time, Gordon picked Clouds House in Wiltshire, another serious therapy centre lumbered with a frothy celebrity reputation. (Robbie Williams, for example, says it got him off drugs in his post-Take That days.) As with the sessions at the Priory five years earlier, Gordon was called on to play a full part in the recovery process. In the autumn of 2004, he would quietly leave his London restaurants and television commitments behind for the drive down to Wiltshire so that he could sit in on the group and individual therapy sessions Ronnie was involved in. And once more it was harrowing stuff.

In previous therapy sessions with Ronnie, Gordon had been told he had just as driven and addictive a personality as his brother. The only difference was the direction in which this relentless nature had been channelled. With Ronnie, it had been towards the destructiveness of drugs and all the illegal activities that go with them. With Gordon, everything had been focused upon his work, his reputation, his status and his achievements. In a nutshell, Gordon was told, he was obsessed with proving his self-worth. Having spent a lifetime thinking he had failed his father, he was now addicted to perfection, the experts said.

Whatever he had felt about this revelation at the time, Gordon was forced to face up to it again when Ronnie attended Clouds House. And he had to do it in public. 'I had to stand up in front of a doctor, a psychiatrist and about 15 recovering addicts and say, "My name is Gordon

Ramsay and I am an addict." It was a humbling experience. I talked to them for two minutes about what I readily admit is my own serious addiction. That I am addicted to perfection.'

Strange as it sounds, the medical view was that Gordon was also addicted to pleasing people. Desperate to make his father happy as a child, psychologists said, he had never lost his desire to be liked by everyone else – and this actually explained the unpleasant behaviour in his kitchens and on television. The theory was that, by shouting and swearing at his staff during service, Gordon was subconsciously making sure that they would pay him compliments afterwards by saying he was 'a decent bloke' or that 'he's a million times nicer' when the heat was off.

Doctors said it was the same with complete strangers. The worse Gordon behaves on television, the more likely it is that people will say they like him when they meet him in person. By lowering people's expectations of him to the level of the gutter, the psychologists said, Gordon ensured he would always come out looking better than his reputation and win the compliments and warmth he had never got from his father. Driving out of Clouds that autumn, Gordon had a lot to think about as his brother's treatment progressed.

And in subsequent therapy sessions that year, Gordon found that his own quest for perfection and praise had inadvertently pushed Ronnie back on to drugs in the past. It was a horrifying lesson to learn. 'I hadn't realised how hard it had been for him,' Gordon said afterwards, his voice slower and quieter than anyone who heard him speak in a kitchen would ever recognise. 'He used to tell me how awful it was for him, with me being so successful. But I used to think it was just addict's talk and wasn't really prepared to listen. Then he started saying, "You know, your success has been hard to deal with. It put me in hiding, made me hibernate." I knew then that he really did need to talk about it and that I needed to listen.'

Fortunately, every worrying, sometimes humiliating, moment of the ten-day detox programme and all the subsequent work proved to be worth it in the end. The still-skeletal Ronnie had at last managed to put on some weight, rather than continuing to lose it. And, when Gordon finally drove his brother out of Clouds, Mark was ready to step in for the next part of the recovery process.

'They just went everywhere together as planned and it worked,' said Gordon, jubilant. In a strange kind of way the full-on, full-time support Mark was offering Ronnie was similar to the equally all-encompassing guidance and direction Gordon had received from the likes of Marco Pierre White, the Roux brothers, Joel Robuchon and Guy Savoy when he had been working 16-hour days with them in their London and Paris kitchens. Having what was in effect a father figure, an experienced, enthusiastic mentor to look up to and learn from, seemed to work wonders for the Ramsay boys. It was just that in Ronnie's case they were finding this out a little later than they all should have done. And everyone had their fingers crossed that Ronnie's amazing progress could be sustained. 'Gordon had lost the brother he once had,' Tana had said, as the latest attempt to rescue him unfolded. 'But hopefully he is coming back.'

This change couldn't have been proved more effectively than when Ronnie at last felt well enough to take his nephew and nieces to a football match in London while Gordon was away filming in America. 'He took all three of them in the car, went to the football, got them an orange juice and a muffin for breakfast. I would never have thought it possible 12 months ago,' said Gordon, unable to hide his pleasure. And soon it wasn't to be just football that linked the brothers again. A love of food was to bring them full circle as well.

Following in Mark's footsteps, Ronnie elected to do some Voluntary Service Overseas charity work as well. In early 2005, he headed east to help with the massive Tsunami relief effort in Thailand. And Gordon says he had to laugh when he found out what job his little brother had been offered out there – and how much he seemed to be enjoying it. 'He's working as a fucking cook, for fuck's sake!' Gordon told friends, tears sometimes forming in his eyes at how perfect it all was. 'He's serving food from the back of a lorry on some island. On the phone he starts talking to me about all these exotic ingredients and how he is grating fresh coconut into Thai curry and I'm thinking, Wow, that sounds nice, I want to do that too.'

Helen Ramsay said receiving news of her recovering son was 'like winning the lottery'. And everyone in the family was looking forward to seeing the changes in the man they had once given up on. 'Being out there has brought a sense of justice to Ronnie's life. His confidence has come back. He has got fit, stopped smoking, his eyes are bright blue, he has got a girlfriend now. It's fantastic,' Gordon said.

On a less kindly note, Gordon reckoned he had something else to smile about as Ronnie's recovery gathered strength: the fact that ITV's *Hell's Kitchen* wasn't doing very well without him. As far as Gordon was concerned, the fun had begun as soon as the producers started scouting around for a replacement presenter. Early rumours said his old rival Antony Worrall Thompson was being considered for the job. Gordon says he could hardly stop laughing at the prospect. 'Worrall Thompson is nowhere near hellish enough,' he began. 'Maybe if he grows another five foot so he can reach the hotplate he'll stand a chance.'

In the end, the producers decided that without Gordon in charge they would have to dramatically change the format of the show to make it work. Out went the celebrity hopefuls, in came members of the public wanting to make it as chefs. And out went the single host and lead chef, as ITV decided that in the 2005 show they would have two chefs in charge and selected Gary Rhodes and Jean-Christophe Novelli for the task. Gordon was unimpressed from the start.

'For me it clearly didn't work with two chefs because there is only one boss in the kitchen – there's never been two bosses. In 2004, *Hell's Kitchen* was an amazing two weeks for me but I didn't ever see it as a programme, I saw it as running a restaurant. And I think everyone could see that I treated that restaurant as I would my own. That was the one fundamental mistake that Gary and Jean-Christophe made. They fell in love with the show and not the objective of running a top-class restaurant. It was also clear that they were letting sub-standard dishes leave the kitchen. I don't think it was as real as when I did it. Twice the number of chefs, half the number of viewers, so draw your own conclusions.'

In all honesty, Gordon had to admit that it was only really his ego that cared whether or not *Hell's Kitchen* had succeeded without him. His bank balance was managing very well without it because, while Gary and Jean-Christophe had been auditioning for his old role, he had been busy selling the show's format to America. As his 38th birthday approached he was about to cross the Atlantic and try to crack the most lucrative entertainment market in the world.

SEVENTEEN

GET READY, AMERICA

Gordon was sitting by the sparkling blue pool at the A-list Chateau Marmont Hotel, just off Sunset Boulevard in Los Angeles. Hours earlier, he had been at Robbie Williams's LA house, chewing the cud and kicking a football around the singer's vast back garden. Later that day, he would have a drink at the hotel bar with Matt Damon before joking along with chat-show host Jay Leno on the *Tonight Show*. It was all a long way from the tenement blocks of Glasgow and the council estates of Stratford-upon-Avon.

Gordon was in Hollywood for one more set of meetings before the American *Hell's Kitchen* finally began filming, and everyone involved was nervous. If the show succeeded and his contract was renewed, Gordon stood to collect a staggering $1 million for a month's work over each of the next five years. Not a bad little wage for someone whose first overseas job in Paris had paid him less than £100 a week and forced him to wait at tables to make ends meet. And, while Gordon admits that money was the major factor that persuaded him to accept the American job, he didn't actually want it to spend on fast cars or wild living. The idea was to pour as much as possible back into Gordon Ramsay Holdings to fund a stream of new Michelin-star-winning restaurants around the world. Even from his Hollywood pool, Gordon had a game plan in place.

But, before he could rely on this new income stream, he had to find out whether the team really could turn a hit British show into a stateside success. The producers of TV hits such as *Coupling*, *Cold Feet* and *Men Behaving Badly* could attest that a lot can be lost in translation when the attempt is made. So the pressure was on and, while the budget was high, so too were the stakes.

In the early days, when he had first begun speaking to the Fox executives about *Hell's Kitchen*, the idea had been to pretty much replicate the British show. A series of meetings took place with Hollywood agents and a stellar cast of hopeful celebrity chefs was put together. Actress Cybill Shepherd was one of the early names mentioned and at one point even ex-President Bill Clinton was marked down as a possible player.

But Gordon was beginning to have second thoughts about the whole concept of teaching famous – or formerly famous – names. 'All those celebrities desperately trying to relaunch their careers…' He fell silent, almost in horror at the thought of going through the same problems in America as he had in Britain. But, if he was to be coaching ordinary members of the public instead of celebrities, he thought the show would need some other extra ingredient to spice it up. Fox was happy to come up with an idea. The contestants would indeed be real people. But the winner wouldn't just walk away with a 'Best Chef' title, having donated some money to charity, as they had in Britain. In America, the winner would get the keys to the $2-million restaurant itself. It would be like winning a culinary lottery and Gordon loved the idea from the start.

The restaurant in question was a former television news studio on La Brea Boulevard in the LA suburb of Willoughby. Over the past two months it had been fitted out as the kitchen, restaurant and accommodation block for the show. On the driveway outside, the obligatory red carpet would be rolled out when the first group of diners arrived – their cars being valet-parked, of course. And Gordon's own tough-talking reputation was being pushed to the maximum as the countdown to the first episode began. 'He's world-renowned – and he's terrifying,' said the billboards. 'His show is dramatic, unscripted and he serves helpings of terror, tears, tantrums and triumphs. Ramsay will slice and dice his contestants. They will be tossed into the cauldron, working under Ramsay and fighting for survival.' And forget the 'Demon Eyes' scandal in Britain when the Conservative Party was attacked for its posters which made Tony Blair look like the devil. The icily scary blue eyes on the massive promotional posters of Gordon Ramsay in America made Tony look like Bambi.

And Gordon was ready to let rip the moment the cameras were rolling. After a huge amount of internal debate, Fox had accepted that bad language was likely to be part of the Ramsay deal. 'It's just as well because I can't change the way I am or the way I work. I would have walked away right at the beginning if they had started any of that "Let's tone things down" bollocks,' Gordon said of the decision.

The other difference between the British and American versions of the show was the way they were filmed and broadcast. The British idea of two weeks of live daily shows had been rejected by the more perfectionist Americans. Instead, they wanted time to edit down the footage from a month's worth of filming, before putting the well-polished result on screen. Instead of cooking every night, the Americans would be cooking every other day, if that. And there would be less real instruction in America. The amateur chefs would be able to focus far more on their own choice of dishes, however simple they were. The idea of trying to replicate Gordon's more complex creations was dismissed. 'We made it clear that this would not be a foodie show,' said Paul Jackson, head of LA's Granada America, which was producing what many saw as a 'dumbed-down' show for Fox. 'In the British version, the splitting of some lobster ravioli became a major talking point. That is not what this show is going to be about.'

With the month-long filming schedule completed and the editing done, the first show hit American screens on Memorial Day weekend, the official start of the American summer, when huge numbers of people switch off their televisions and head outside or into the country. Ratings were decent, if unspectacular. But, as Gordon's behaviour started to get talked about, Fox got the audience lift it had been hoping for. By the time the two-hour finale was aired, *Hell's Kitchen* was the top-rated show of the week in the 18–49 age bracket that television companies – and their advertisers – are desperate to attract. Gordon Ramsay had become a household name, of which a lot more later.

In the first episode, with its opening shots of the night-time LA skyline, Gordon started as he meant to go on. Having arrived at the restaurant, the 12 contestants had 45 minutes to make their signature dishes, which 'Chef Ramsay' proceeded to dissect. Andrew, a 24-year-old office assistant from Livingston, New Jersey, was first to step forward for the analysis. And very soon he wished he hadn't.

Gordon tasted the pasta dish, grimaced, leaned to his side and spat the mouthful out into a bucket. 'That is absolute dog shit' was his initial conclusion. But the transcript shows there was another shock to come.

'Have a taste,' he challenged Andrew.

'It could use some salt,' the trainee chef replied.

'You think you're smart, yeah?'

'I have my moments.'

'And how long have you been cooking?'

'Ten years.'

'What a waste of ten years. Get back in fucking line.'

So there it was: the first f-word of the show. A massive shock for American television audiences. The country's squeamishness about what goes on television has long surprised Europeans, who could never really understand why such a fuss was made after Janet Jackson's 'wardrobe malfunction' at the 2004 Super Bowl. That one brief flash of Jackson's flesh had triggered public apologies by television network chiefs and a huge fine and led to the introduction of time delays on similar broadcasts in the future. So no one could quite believe that Gordon could get away with such unwholesome language on a prime-time reality show. But somehow he did and, as *Hell's Kitchen* continued, the insults and the honesty would continue to fly.

'If I had known you were coming, I would have put lobster in,' said one of the next contestants after Gordon tasted her signature dish of Chinese sausage.

'You did know I was coming. Get back in line' was all it took to dismiss her.

And then there was the glorious-sounding 'pan-seared chicken breast, stuffed with Portobello mushrooms and goat's cheese' from 25-year-old purchasing manager Jimmy from Williston Park, New York. 'It looks like a dehydrated camel's turd' was Gordon's description, before that sample too was spat into the bin and Gordon started throwing some of the food back at its creator to see if he was agile enough to catch it. He wasn't, which led to another shock for American audiences.

Gordon was also ready to speak his mind about a different television taboo: size. 'For as long as Jimmy weighs 250 pounds, he is never going to make a great chef because he is too clumsy' was Gordon's initial verdict on the contestant he would endlessly refer to as 'big boy' and once as 'one big, fucking overgrown muffin'.

Next up was 26-year-old Ralf, whose job, he said, was 'Number One in a restaurant'. Gordon was unimpressed. 'Number One? With this shit? Back in line' was all he needed to say.

The contestants soon learned that answering back was a bad idea – as proved by Colorado chef Michael. 'It's really not that bad,' the 27-year-old countered feebly, after his dish was rejected.

'Not that bad? Let me tell you something, you have a palate like a cow's backside, that was disgusting,' he was told.

Gordon's overall verdict when every dish had been tasted was not good: 'a pile of shit' was just one other pithy description. But he repeated his belief that anyone could be transformed into a master chef with the right instruction, encouragement and passion. He would do so with at least one member of this group. And since he had scattered a few compliments among the criticisms it was possible to believe him.

Off set and off camera, what Gordon couldn't believe was the way the American contestants seemed to have been shielded from the truth all their lives. 'In my London restaurants, if someone makes a mistake there can be no: "Hey, let's sit down and discuss this, and never mind, you'll get it right next time,"' he said. But, as Simon Cowell had found when filming *American Idol*, 'never mind, you'll get it right next time' seemed to be the American way. Genuine criticism seemed off limits, with everyone desperate to accentuate the positive and gloss over any shortcomings. In LA, negativity seemed to be a bigger sin than swearing and Gordon reckoned his hopeful chefs had been over-praised for too long. On his television debut there, he wanted to give everyone a very loud wake-up call.

Unfortunately, within days of starting the show, Gordon was to get a wake-up call himself. A very minor scuffle took place off camera when Gordon got too close to one of his trainees, who then stumbled back and injured his ankle. In most parts of the world, it would have been bad luck, soon forgotten. In America, it triggered a legal crisis that threatened to bring production of the show to a shuddering halt – much to Gordon's disgust. 'The problem with Yanks is that they are just wimps' was his conclusion on the matter. 'I've never punched anyone in a kitchen, but I have been punched. You stand there like a man, you don't wimp out and run crying for your mum. In America, they run for their attorney. I'm Gordon Ramsay, for goodness sake. People know I'm volatile. But I didn't mean to hurt the guy.'

The injured contestant allegedly wanted to sue Gordon and his producers for $3 million but after a series of meetings Granada was said to have sorted the matter out with a $125,000 out-of-court settlement. Other experts said Gordon and Granada might have been putting themselves in line for a different set of legal problems owing to the confrontational nature of the show. 'Back in Britain, a barrage of criticism and insults could undermine an employee's confidence and lead to accusations of unfair constructive dismissal and big compensation claims,' said Iain Patterson, partner at law firm Browne Jackson. Triggering the same events across the Atlantic in the most litigious country on earth was not worth contemplating. So lawyers, on all sides, were kept busy for the duration of Gordon's stay.

The final group of people who were open-mouthed at Gordon's attitudes and language were the hopeful diners who came to *Hell's Kitchen* expecting a decent meal. They were in the most service-driven economy in the world, confident that in America the customer was always king.

Or at least that is the way things had been until now. In Gordon's little corner of America, the head chef was king – and the customer had to wait until the chef was happy before they got their food.

'Can you just shut the fuck up for 30 seconds?' he yelled at three blonde women who had been waiting more than 45 minutes for their starters and very reasonably came into the kitchen to ask when they might be arriving. 'Just ignore those bimbos,' he told his staff as the women gave up and returned to their table. An hour and a quarter later, when the foursome had been served their starters but were still waiting for their main courses, they came back to the chef's window again – for a second slice of classic Ramsay.

'Mr Chef, you hurt my friend's feelings,' one of them began, again perfectly reasonably.

'I hurt your friend's feelings? How?' Gordon asked, unable even to pretend that he cared.

'She is very upset because you told her to fuck off.'

'Oh really, did I? OK, will you tell her that I meant it?' was his perfect putdown before asking the maitre d' to 'escort these women back to plastic surgery'.

The two American chefs who were heading up the red and blue teams in America admitted to being staggered at the way Gordon spoke and acted from the first moment they met. 'The first time I was introduced to him, he was clearly the biggest guy in the room,' said Scott Leibfried, himself a bruiser of a chef whose day job was at the celebrated Napa Valley Grill in Los Angeles. 'I haven't heard stuff like he is dishing out in a very long time. In the state of California, that sort of thing is actually illegal. You can't cuss at your staff.'

But, as Gordon cussed away, the jury was still out on whether the show would be a hit. At first, the American critics were unimpressed, just as the British ones had been. 'It's a cooking show that's hard to stomach,' said the *Washington Post* amid a sea of equally negative culinary cliches. 'Ramsay is a cartoonishly abusive snot,' said the show-business bible *Variety*. But, as the episodes rolled by and the trainee chefs shaped up, viewers were starting to love the show. Gordon had picked up the nickname G-Ram and was starting to become a household name. Or at least he was in households where swearing was allowed, which seemed to be an awful lot more than some straight-laced critics had imagined. Mike Darnell, one of the senior executives at the Fox network, said Ramsay's 'acerbic' style was the peg that had helped get American viewers hooked. So after the heavily tattooed chef Michael had won the show – getting an offer to work at Gordon Ramsay in London as part of the package – the man himself was immediately signed up for a second big-money series.

And the money certainly was big. Simon Cowell, Anne Robinson and even tough 'Supernanny' Jo Frost have all found that speaking your mind in America can do wonders for your bank account. Gordon had been edging his way towards inclusion in most of the newspaper Rich Lists for the past five years. By the summer of 2004, he was valued at £20 million and hit eighteenth position in the list of Britain's wealthiest 'craft millionaires' – people who had made it to the top without going to university. Top of that list was Phones 4U founder John Caudwell with a hard-to-beat fortune of £1.28 billion. By 2006, Gordon had made it on to the mainstream rich lists, however, and this wasn't just due to the entertainment money coming in from America.

When the cameras were not rolling at home and abroad, Gordon had been busy expanding almost every other aspect of his culinary empire. The core restaurants were still working as strong cash generators: in 2005, it was revealed that his Claridge's site was making a profit of nearly £1.5 million a year after nearly £7 million went through its tills in just 12 months. The Savoy Grill and the Gordon Ramsay restaurant were each making profits of more than £400,000 a year and Petrus added nearly £300,000 to the cash pile. Ramsay restaurants at the Connaught and Berkeley Hotels also made profits of more than £13,000 a month. In the year in which losses of up to £800,000 from the closure of Amaryllis in Glasgow were still being absorbed, Gordon's holding company still made a record profit of some £3.8 million, with analysts saying the whole business could be worth a staggering £50 million.

While all the cash tills had been ringing, Gordon had turned into a major employer – his staff numbers rise by at least a hundred a year, depending on the number of restaurant launches, and topped one thousand by the middle of 2005. But what got the accountants really excited were all the spin-off business ventures that added millions more to Gordon's total income. And these were about as varied as you can imagine. Gordon's willingness to keep taking his shirt off during *Ramsay's Kitchen Nightmares* had won him a surprising new fan base, so the tired-looking 38-year-old took the unexpected step of posing for his own glossy calendar in 2005. Flatteringly, he saw it outsell many of the more predictably popular offerings from the likes of Peter Andre, the '*Hollyoaks* Babes' and the 'Soap Hunks'.

Gordon was also estimated to sell up to £4 million a year of his own-label chocolates, even though these had been launched pretty much on a whim and never given any proper publicity or marketing. A signature line of fine bone china was being planned and a new range of ready meals for supermarkets was being considered.

A subtle change of direction had also given Gordon's publishing income a boost. His early cookbooks – *A Passion for Flavour*, *A Passion for Seafood*, *A Chef for All Seasons* and *Just Desserts* – had come in for some widespread criticism for demanding too much of their readers. The public perception was that the books sometimes read like instructional manuals and didn't make cooking seem much fun because when you tried to follow the recipes you spent too much time worrying you might be getting things wrong. And Gordon's schoolmasterly attitude seemed out of step in an era when the likes of Jamie Oliver and Nigella Lawson were hamming it up, showing that exact measurements didn't always matter and that almost anyone could make good food. Conspiracy theorists said that Gordon deliberately made his early books overly complicated so that readers would make mistakes at home and end up spending big money in his restaurants to see how things should really be done.

Gordon Ramsay's Kitchen Heaven was Gordon's first attempt to boost book sales and redress the balance. First published in 2004, it was unashamedly linked to the *Kitchen Nightmares* show and included a brief mention of many of the good and bad things he had seen while filming. It included more than a hundred new recipes but, despite Gordon's attempts at a lighter touch, some buyers continued to be turned off by the overall tone.

'It is an interesting if a bit light on content cookbook,' wrote one London-based reviewer on Amazon. 'A short word of warning though to less-than-confident cooks. Many of the recipes assume a reasonable level of culinary skill which may have some starters a bit lost. Delia Smith it ain't.'

Another reviewer agreed that Gordon's book came off worse than Delia's in the value-for-money stakes when the number of recipes in each was added up. Others repeated the old claims that the recipes were made unnecessarily hard just to try to make the chef who created them look good.

Having taken comments such as these on board, Gordon finally came up with a very lucrative back-to-basics response: *Gordon Ramsay Makes It Easy*. The idea was to write a book that would 'do what it says on the tin' and bring a whole new generation of nervous cooks into his fold. In a bid to create the practical, real-world edge that people said had been missing from his early books, Gordon and his team researched and wrote the new book in his family kitchen. It was a bit of an eye-opener for a man who had got used to the most lavish restaurant kitchens money can buy. 'It's hard, cooking at home,' he admitted when he talked about these latest recipes. 'You've got no brigade. You have to prep, cook and wash up and the space is limited. You have to be more clever in buying the ingredients because you've got less refrigerator space. Recipes have to reflect all this.'

And it turned out that the new, simpler ideas did just that. The book hit the hardback top ten within weeks of its publication in 2005 and became his best selling book to date. And this wasn't the only money Gordon was making from publishing his recipes. He had signed what was thought to be the best-paid newspaper deal in Fleet Street when he agreed to produce an average of three colour pages of recipes and comment for *The Times*'s Saturday magazine each week. No one has said publicly how much his contract was worth. But industry experts put it at around £2,500 a week – or £500 per well-photographed recipe.

With so much going on, it was little wonder that Gordon increasingly started to rely on others to run huge parts of his life. 'Chefs are the worst businessmen in the world,' he said once. 'I have never made the mistake of believing that I am a chef and a businessman at the same time. That way trouble lies – the two just don't mix.' Trusting his entire financial affairs to his father-in-law, Chris, left Gordon free to focus on his new set of career mountains in America and beyond. It was a policy that had paid huge dividends in recent years. But as 2005 got under way, both Gordon and Chris faced a series of warnings that the gravy train might not run for ever.

The first came when a newspaper used the new Freedom of Information Act to obtain documents proving that the ill-fated Amaryllis in Glasgow had failed basic hygiene and cleaning tests before being closed down. Meanwhile, critics were circling over several of Gordon's more successful London restaurants with claims that they were starting to lose their spark. But the most worrying rumours of all suggested that at least some of Gordon's hard-won Michelin stars could be at risk if he carried on playing for the cameras around the world and left his kitchens to fend for themselves.

It was serious stuff and Gordon and Chris knew they had to tackle it straight away. Television and America would have to go on hold for a while, Gordon decided. For the next few months, he had work to do in London.

EIGHTEEN
NO LIMITS

'Stay close to the kitchen.' That had been the simple piece of advice Gordon had been given as a fiercely ambitious 20-something trainee chef in Paris. Back in London in the early summer of 2005, he knew he had to start living up to it again. Over the past few months, a series of unflattering reviews of his flagship restaurants had been published and posted on internet websites. It looked as if his prolonged absences from the restaurants that bore his name were starting to cause problems and it was feared that the consequences could be far more serious than they looked.

With massively high fixed costs, Gordon was acutely aware that once restaurants hit the skids they can fail faster than almost any other business. And he knew that once customers lose faith in a restaurant they hardly ever come back.

'To me, Gordon was my god until I ate here,' a Moya King wrote on one website about his eponymous Chelsea restaurant. 'Food was lacking any of the passion I expected, celeriac soup was a creamy glue, two courses back to back contained peas and broad beans, desserts were not pleasant, panna cotta was tasteless and chocolate tarte so bitter I couldn't eat it, and service was lacking any kind of warmth and leadership. After hearing all he preaches on television Gordon would not have been happy dining with me that evening. Save your money,' she advised other diners.

But a worrying number of other people already seemed to share Moya's opinions. 'Not the best place we have been to. I was expecting one hundred per cent for the price we were paying but service wasn't up to standard, the food was just OK and the desserts were naff. Won't be going there again, sorry, Gordon,' came from Anna O'Neill towards the end of June 2005.

'I had the set lunch and as a former restaurant reviewer I have to say that this is not extraordinary cooking,' wrote another diner, while phrases such as 'Too expensive and too pretentious', 'No atmosphere and the food was average', 'Not worth the money you are spending' and 'This proves that hype can override quality' littered a host of other customer comments that summer.

Over the years, Gordon had been criticised by everyone from broadcasting standards officers to cookery school teachers. None of it had bothered him. 'I will only start worrying if my customers start complaining,' he said in the late 1990s. Nearly a decade later, having read some of the comments while surfing the web in the offices deep within Claridge's Hotel, Gordon wondered if that time had finally come. He walked down to the staff toilets and passed the BAFTA award he had won the previous April for his performance in *Ramsay's Kitchen Nightmares*. Collecting it had been a fantastic honour. But no amount of entertainment gongs would dull the pain if he lost some of his even more valuable Michelin stars.

'Don't judge me, judge my food,' he had once said in defiance of a critic who said his x-rated diatribes on television were dragging the industry down. But could he in all honesty say he was as involved in that food in 2005 as he had been five or ten years earlier?

Fortunately, two recent incidents had reminded Gordon that his love of kitchen life was as strong as ever. The first had become apparent in America during the filming of *Hell's Kitchen* – the very thing that was being blamed for letting his mind wander. 'It was doing the nightly service at *Hell's Kitchen*. It was torture, but it was self-inflicted torture. I realised that the last time it had felt like that to me had been in the early days of Aubergine when it was chaotic. I like that roughness. I need to feel that stuff. It's back to school, the challenge is there, there's the struggle to get it right which I hadn't felt for two or three years. It was all the old questions of what everyone on the team was thinking, how they are feeling, who is going to fuck up, who is going to perform. I realised I missed the adrenalin, I missed that kind of buzz,' he said immediately afterwards.

The second reminder came when he came back from a brief 'boyfriend and girlfriend' holiday with Tana. 'When we landed I thought, It will be so nice to see the kids, I can't wait. But I just saw them for 15 minutes and then I went back to work. It was only after I had been back in the kitchen at Claridge's for 20 minutes that I started to mellow out and feel I was coming back to life again.'

Desperate to keep these feelings alive and to kick-start his restaurants, Gordon went on a whistle-stop midsummer tour of his kitchens and dining rooms across the capital. And he immediately realised that he had to regain control over the way his restaurants felt, as well as over what they served. One of the reasons he said Amaryllis in Glasgow had lost money and been forced to close was because he felt the head chef there had got too carried away with making fancy, self-indulgent food that confused and intimidated potential customers. If there was any danger of this trend being repeated in London, he realised he would have to act fast to nip it in the bud.

As a man born and brought up on a council estate, Gordon had always been determined to make sure that people from a similar background could feel comfortable in every one of his restaurants. 'I have always hated all that pompous, farty intimidation stuff that you used to get in every hotel restaurant in the world. I had to change all that in mine,' he says. And he thinks fair and impeccable service is the best way to make sure these changes stick. In a Ramsay restaurant, he says, everyone has to be treated the same and everyone has to be treated well – and after a few weeks back in the London hot seats he was certain he was fulfilling the promise. 'This month I have served Kylie Minogue, George Clooney and my little sister. They all got the same treatment as every other customer. The other day a couple from Yorkshire also came all the way down to London to eat lunch at one of my London restaurants for £70, accompanied by a carafe of tap water. They were treated no differently from any so-called VIP client or the businessmen who once spent £44,000 on dinner at Petrus.'

That said, a few favoured customers did qualify for a little extra attention. When *Ramsay's Kitchen Nightmares*' Charita Jones and her family came to his flagship restaurant in Claridge's to celebrate her foster daughter's 21st birthday she enjoyed a special welcome. 'Gordon sent bottles of Champagne to us and treated us like royalty,' says Charita, whose Brighton restaurant was still thriving more than a year after Gordon had arrived to troubleshoot it.

Sitting alone at Claridge's after another late-night service had ended, Gordon took stock of the state of play in his own business. There had, perhaps, been shortcomings in some of the attitudes and standards he had seen over the past few weeks. But he was convinced he had managed to deal with the worst of them and re-inspire his staff about what they could and should be achieving. He was confident that his teams were back at the top of their games. And that was important, because the Ramsay empire was in for yet another massive period of expansion. It would be some time before Gordon could spend so much time in his kitchens again.

On 25 May 2005, for example, when the first show in the second series of *Ramsay's Kitchen Nightmares* had been broadcast on Channel 4, Gordon hadn't had time to watch. Instead, he had been hoping to see the Beckhams and a host of other celebrity invitees at the launch of Maze, his eighth London restaurant. Billed as a New York-style diner, Maze is squeezed into the Marriott Hotel in Grosvenor Square, just around the corner from the heavily fortified American Embassy.

The idea behind the restaurant was a real departure from the relatively formal dining structures at Gordon's other hotel restaurants. Instead of choosing a standard starter, main course and dessert, diners at Maze pick any number of small 'tapas-style' dishes at around £11 a time. Gordon said he was fusing French and Asian cuisine on the menu, which included the likes of foie gras and apricot pizza, lamb with cinnamon roasted sweetbreads and bay leaf and Alsace chard. And, if you fancy an unusual pudding, his sea salt and almond ice cream is pretty hard to beat.

Gordon says that these off-the-wall menu ideas – half of them created in the kitchen in Gordon and Tana's home, half at Claridge's – are what keeps him enthusiastic about food and what drives him to keep opening new restaurants. A dish of scallops with a spiced raisin puree and cauliflower might not work at Gordon Ramsay in Chelsea, for example. But, in opening Maze, Gordon reckoned he and his head chef, Jason Atherton, had found somewhere suitable to serve it.

Gordon has always been a voracious consumer of information about what other chefs are doing, and at home he has stacks of boxes where he files his 3,500-strong (and growing) collection of menus from around the world. 'Whenever I hear from a guest in one of my restaurants that they are going somewhere new I ask if they might get me a menu,' he says. 'One of my favourites is from the three-Michelin-star Louis XV in Monaco.'

He will also spend big money checking out the competition. 'Any time a good new restaurant opens up, anywhere in the world, we check it out,' he told a London management conference which had asked him to share his business secrets. 'Five years ago, we could afford to do this just in Britain. But now, to stay in front, we have to respond to the amazing changes happening in, say, Asia and Australia. I send teams of four to six people to these places, not just chefs but waiters too, and they check out everything, even delicatessens and cooking stores. Then we start incorporating the best ideas into what we do.'

Not surprisingly, the man who says he has no time to read books, except for the occasional sporting biography, also keeps tabs on the industry through a vast collection of rival cookbooks. And in 2005 he needed all the new ideas he could lay his hands on.

Having conquered American television screens, Gordon was searching for a site in New York so that he could try to conquer the famously demanding diners of Manhattan. But before that he had another huge challenge, amid the equally expensive skyscrapers of Tokyo. The Japanese job had come to Gordon via Jan Monkedieck, the German general manager of the brand-new and extraordinarily luxurious Conrad Toyko Hotel. 'Within minutes of learning that I would be running the hotel, I knew I had to get Gordon,' says Jan. So Gordon grabbed some red-eye flights to the Far East to discuss the opening of the 80-seater restaurant Cerise by Gordon Ramsay. In the process, he tried to defy the critics who said he was only a figurehead to vanity projects that borrowed his name but neither his time nor his attention. Furnishing a dining room could be as satisfying as furnishing a plate, he said. And, to the joy of his fellow professionals, he could be just as demanding of both tasks.

'There is nothing worse than someone saying, "I want a

restaurant. Let me know when it's finished," and walking away,' says designer and Ramsay client Keith Hobbs, of United Designers, who helped Terence Conran design the massive Quaglino's restaurant and has since worked with most rival restaurateurs. 'It helps if clients make a real commitment to a project and that's why we like working with Gordon Ramsay and others such as Marco Pierre White. They do show the commitment, they know what they want and they know how to run a restaurant.'

In Tokyo, running a restaurant takes even more skill and care, however. The whole culture of Japan is based on doing things right, so an extraordinary attention to detail is required if you are to succeed there. And in 2005 Gordon was not the only big-name chef trying to make a mark in the Far East. Once more, he would find himself competing against a former mentor, this time Joel Robuchon, who had an established luxury restaurant in the city.

Convinced that his name would win more attention, and generate more yen, Gordon put his head down and continued to work on the launch. He admitted that the language barriers in the kitchen were causing difficulties and that the humidity was causing problems with the desserts. But he said both challenges were exciting rather than insurmountable. As usual, Gordon's strategy was to take a near-obsessive control of the set-up stages of the new venture, before handing over the reins to one of his young lieutenants, in this case 28-year-old Chelsea and Claridge's graduate Andy Cook.

What Gordon did, with shades of Richard Branson and easyJet's Stelios, was ham things up to win headlines when the opening night arrived: he wore a flowing Japanese cape and happily smashed open the traditional barrel of sake for luck. In his typical unrestrained style, Gordon was also ready to shout down any of his critics who said he was spreading himself too thinly and that standards in Cerise would drop the moment he left Japan.

'If you're such a hands-on chef, who's going to do the cooking when you are not there?' This time it was an American journalist who asked the question during the launch celebrations in Tokyo.

'The same person who is going to do it when I am there. And can I ask you a question? Is that an Armani suit you are wearing?'

'Yes it is.'

'Cost about five hundred quid?'

'No, $2,500.'

'That's a lot of money for a suit. When you bought it, did you ask if it was fucking Giorgio who did all the stitching? Next question.'

The press conference, Gordon says, didn't last much longer, and with his point made he shook Andy by the hand one more time and left him to follow his training, spin the Ramsay magic and hopefully win some fantastic reviews. Gordon himself had more work to do elsewhere.

On his way back from Tokyo, Gordon got a little more than the standard mealtime question 'Chicken or beef, sir?' from the cabin crew. He got the chance to choose from half a dozen of his own meals, each of which had been created as part of a lucrative and long-term deal to oversee the Business and First Class catering of Singapore Airlines. The restaurants in Dubai and now Tokyo meant that you could eat Gordon's food in the Middle and the Far East as well as in Europe. The Singapore Airlines deal meant you could eat it as you travelled between each of the territories. Getting his name above a door in New York, Las Vegas or Miami would put yet another continent under Gordon's belt. And as he headed back to London this was to be his next big challenge.

'It has always been my ambition to come to America and open a restaurant. But you've only got one shot at it, so you have to get it right,' Gordon said, as the search for a perfect site went on. He was acutely aware that few British chefs had made a real go of things in the States. So, as usual, he wanted to be the one to do it first and then break the mould. Getting the food right to succeed in America would be as important as getting the location right, however. And it was here that Gordon was hitting some unexpected difficulties.

Nearly two decades earlier, as a hard-up trainee chef, Gordon had been unable to afford to check out the competition by visiting any of the great restaurants. Now, with millions in the bank, his problem was eating out without being hassled by other diners and the master chefs themselves. 'Eating out can be a pain in the arse. Nowadays I tend to get offered four or five courses I don't want. It's kind of the chefs, but they always ask your opinion. The minute you don't finish a dish completely, the chef wants to know what it was about his food you didn't like. I'm flattered they offer me all these dishes but to be honest I always end up waiting 45 minutes for my starter and then another hour for my main course,' he said of his experiences eating out in Britain. Since *Hell's Kitchen* had gone on national television in America, the same was happening on that side of the Atlantic. 'Everything's gone wild over there and I can't get off the plane without people wanting to talk to or own a part of me.'

Not surprisingly, Gordon says the biggest problems arise in his own restaurants – effectively making their dining rooms off limits for him. 'I know that I would lose all respect from my staff and customers if they turned around and saw me overindulging, and the diners in particular want to see me downstairs cooking their food rather than sitting with them eating it,' he says wistfully. 'But it's really weird to be in this situation as they are good restaurants and I would love to eat in them some day.'

Sending Tana out to scout around for him was becoming almost as hard, because her public profile was edging up as well. Having done the obligatory 'at home' shoots for a series of celebrity magazines, she had taken advantage of her skills as a former nursery-school teacher by filming a week-long stint on *GMTV* sharing parenting tips in *Ramsay's Toddler Nightmares*. The idea had been for her to try to help a family run ragged by their badly behaved kids. 'I consider my children well-behaved but they still test my patience now and again, so I am not saying that if I show you ways in which I have dealt with problems that everything will be perfect for you,' Tana began. 'But if you have some basic rules and you're consistent with them you can deal with difficult situations a lot quicker and a lot more easily.' Telly nanny Jo Frost and Dr Tanya Byron could hardly have put it better themselves.

But was this *GMTV* picture a true reflection of family life at the Ramsays'? Tana had to admit that it was a relief that the cameras hadn't been there on any of the many occasions her husband tried to bring their kids into line by threatening to cook their pet rabbit, Daisy, for example. Fortunately, the Ramsay children could always tell when their dad was joking, and they knew exactly how to twist him round their little fingers. A few years earlier, Megan had surprised her pre-school friends by telling them, 'My dad's a cooker.' Now she was well able to distinguish between the 'the yukky man on television' and the big softie who had finally given in to her request for a chocolate-brown Labrador called Dudley, which she helped walk in the five-acre private gardens that backed on to their London home.

What Megan and the other children couldn't do was follow their dad into work. Gordon and Tana were both determined not to raise either food snobs or rich kids who didn't know the value of money. As usual, there was a rash of disapproving publicity when Gordon said his kids were banned from Claridge's and his other restaurants until they were at least 16. Chefs from Europe in particular said that doing so would mean Britain raised another generation of kids who didn't respect good food and didn't know how to behave when they ate out in public.

But Gordon refused to bow to demands for a rethink, and added that high prices meant he wouldn't be taking them for afternoon tea in any grand London hotel either. 'I could never take my children and spend £22 a head just to sit and have afternoon tea, it's not apt, it's wrong and I can't think any differently. My mum would be mortified. Then there's my uncle Ronald, who runs a newsagent in Port Glasgow and gets 3p a paper. What would he think if

I took the kids to a hotel to have afternoon tea for six at those sorts of prices? He would think I had gone mad. My mum still works for social services; my sister is a single parent. I know what it is like to earn £100 a week and pay your rent and save up £50 to take your partner out to dinner. I haven't lost the plot and I don't want anyone else to either.'

With Gordon, however, every relatively serious public pronouncement he makes tends to be followed by a more humorous follow-up. So, after saying his children couldn't dine in his restaurants, he did suggest that if he and Tana had another baby they would all be allowed to get jobs in his kitchens. 'Five kids would be amazing,' he said. 'One each on fish, meat, hot starters, cold starters and the desserts. We could have a whole brigade and run our own restaurant.'

Adding humour to the mix alongside his serious statements is only one characteristic of Gordon's extraordinary life. Another is the fact that, amid all his good times, potential tragedy is never far from the surface. The sudden death of his abusive father, the worst relapses of his drug-addicted brother, the death threats, the death of his best friend. Each awful incident had come at a time when almost everything else in Gordon's life had been going well and he had begun to relax about the future. It was a disturbing and seemingly endless pattern. So a tiny part of him may have been expecting the phone call that came during the brief family holiday he took in the late summer of 2005.

When it came, the news was terrible in itself. But it was even more shocking for the way it echoed the past. The call came through on Gordon's mobile. One of his most senior members of staff, a man who was also one of Gordon's closest friends, had fallen 50 feet from a ledge outside his flat in Stockwell on to the pavement below. Reports said the 30-year-old had been taken unconscious to King's College Hospital in London with a suspected broken back and a long list of possible internal injuries. No one knew if he would survive.

Gordon sat with Tana in shocked silence as they digested the news. The similarities with David Dempsey's death, who had also fallen from a window ledge on the front of a block of flats, were chilling and impossible to ignore. Was history repeating itself? Gordon asked himself, horrified, as he waited for more news from London. Could his great friend possibly have suffered a similar, possibly drug-induced reaction to the one which had helped kill David?

Fortunately, Gordon very quickly found out that there was nothing sinister about this awful accident. No drink or drugs had been involved at all in this second fall. It turned out that the man had just been trying to get into his own flat late at night after leaving his keys at work. He regained consciousness fast and Gordon rang him every 24 hours from his holiday to check on his progress before giving him a huge and tearful telling-off back in London. Gordon had lost too many people he loved to risk losing another through something so stupid as a forgotten set of house keys.

With this tragedy averted, Gordon did have other problems to face in late 2005, however. Like every successful person in Britain, he has faced an almost relentless series of criticisms from people who seem desperate to question his motives or see him fail. What is often at issue is his genuine commitment to food – which cynics say does not ring true for someone who appears on so many television screens. The idea seems to be that in life you can be one thing or another: good at what you do or a television star. The fact that you can be a television star because you are good at what you do seems to pass people by.

Yet asking Gordon just one question about food should prove his knowledge base and his love of the subject are far deeper than his critics allege. 'Nothing is just skin deep when you speak to Gordon about food,' said reporter Tamsin Richie, who spent an afternoon in his kitchen at Claridge's in 2005. 'He has a genuine, overwhelming passion for finding the right ingredients and creating something extraordinary out of them. Details matter enormously to him and he can talk for so long about something as simple as a piece of raw salmon that your own eyes can glaze over while his are still burning. The science of cooking is as important as the flavour he creates. He wants to know why things happen as well as just making them happen. He will wrap you up in his enthusiasm and his new ideas and he simply fails to understand it if you don't share his interest.'

Another writer, the *Observer*'s Nicci Gerrard, made the point even more starkly after she too spent time watching the chef at work. 'Ramsay's bashed-in face, especially when he gets angry, can screw into a grooved and winded exhaustion that looks close to despair. He cares too much about cooking. It's not love so much as obsession.'

But had Gordon found a new love in television that

would push his old passions to the sidelines? The £1.2-million Channel 4 deal he had signed to make more series of *Ramsay's Kitchen Nightmares* included the option to make pretty much any other shows he chose – though everyone expected him to turn all the other proposals down so that he could spend more time in his kitchens.

The broadcaster got a pleasant surprise, then, when Gordon said he was up for a new prime-time magazine-style show called – perhaps naturally – *The F-Word*. The nine-week show was filmed live in the autumn of 2005 and aimed to give another look at what happened in a restaurant's kitchens, bar areas and dining rooms when Gordon took control.

His co-host on the show was the restaurant critic Giles Coren, and sparks flew from the start. 'If people think Gordon is a rude bastard, wait until they hear me' was how Giles put it as the pair launched the series. For his part, Gordon wanted to take the focus from the 'chef idol' element of the production and put the spotlight firmly back on the food. 'We're going undercover and exposing bad service, bad value and bad food on behalf of customers. We're also trying to encourage more women to consider careers in restaurants and keep people up to date with what's going on in the food industry,' he said.

And, to those who said he was once more straying too far from his own kitchens, his response was typically frank. 'Fuck off, it's one night a week. Everyone deserves a night off,' he said dismissively just before the cameras started to roll.

What the new show also proved was that Gordon hadn't yet lost his addiction to adrenalin. Live television is hugely stressful – about as stressful, in fact, as running a Michelin-starred restaurant. So Gordon had seen to it that his nights off continued to be as tense as his nights on.

When he was in his growing family of kitchens Gordon did admit to having mellowed towards many of his former betes noires, however – including picky diners and vegetarians. 'The other day a customer asked for tomato ketchup and I told him to go to Europa Foods. Two years ago, I would have thrown his table out of the window,' he says when asked about the former. When it comes to vegetarians, Gordon is finally prepared to admit he can learn things by leaving the meat in the fridge. 'Two nights ago, I roasted lettuce, in the oven, with a beautiful thyme stock, and it has to be the most amazing dish I have ever eaten. It was for a vegetarian – we have a vegetarian menu in all my restaurants now and this was to die for. It was served with shavings of Parmesan and roasted ceps – beautiful. And the vegetarian lady gave me a big kiss on the lips, because she had never eaten vegetarian food quite like that. That was a big learning curve for me. I am still learning – that's the beauty of my food, I'm still getting better. I still consider myself a cook but it takes years to become a great chef.'

This sort of humility is not what many people expect to hear from a man who has steamrollered through so many challenges on his way to the top. But, for all the clarity of his public persona, Gordon remains the ultimate man of contrasts. He is the foul-mouthed former footballer who says moisturiser would be his 'desert island essential'. He is the multi-millionaire who celebrated his 38th birthday in a fish and chip shop just outside Blackpool. The man who shouts and swears at every member of his staff but ensures even the cleaners in his kitchens get a share of their restaurant's tips. The father who won't watch his children being born but takes them to lunch at a greasy spoon every week to make sure they share quality time with him. The devoted husband who says Elizabeth Hurley is his dream dinner date.

And he is also the man who has taken so much from life but is always prepared to give something back. Last year, a little girl who had just left hospital got a rare glimpse of this private Gordon Ramsay. 'She was 11 years of age, she had a brain tumour and she was totally obsessed with food. She wanted to have a last meal cooked by me but apparently she didn't think I would ever make fish and chips. I said, "Listen, not only am I going to make you fish and chips, I am going to make you the very best fish and chips in the world." She even got ketchup with them and she was so pleased she could hardly speak.'

Gordon's other charitable instincts are not always carried through with the decorum that might be expected, however. Every year he holds a special lunch for the scarlet-jacketed Chelsea Pensioners at his eponymous restaurant in Royal Hospital Road. And some years they get more than they bargain for. 'We love holding this lunch for them but you have to watch them carefully as the years haven't dimmed their amorous appetites,' he says. 'This year I took on five extra waitresses to deal with them and added some Viagra to their pudding.'

It is this kind of irrepressible irreverence that seems to win the public over when his other words and actions seem too arrogant to take. And this is the final contrast that shines through Gordon's life. He won't take himself or anyone else too seriously. But his food must always be treated with the utmost respect. Laugh at me all you like, he challenges the critics. But don't ever dare underestimate how much I care about food.

'The day that I can accept that opening a scallop properly doesn't matter is the day I have to get out of this business,' he said when people first criticised the relentless perfectionism he displayed when he opened Aubergine nearly a decade and a half ago. 'The day that I walk into a kitchen and think of the money and forget my standards is the day I retire.' Fortunately, it looks as if that day is still as far away as ever.

Gordon Ramsay's journey through life has been extraordinary. From a council estate in Glasgow and Ibrox Park football ground through the luxury yachts of Europe, the most expensive restaurants in Paris and London and the television studios of Hollywood. Awarded the OBE in 2006 he has cooked for prime ministers and presidents, raised huge amounts of money for charity and tested himself against the very best in every area of his life. He has seen his mother beaten up, his father and friends die, his brother survive hard drugs and his sisters thrive. He has fallen in love, stayed in love and raised a family that he adores.

Clinically competitive, Gordon has won just about every competition he has ever entered. Yet he remains incapable of turning down new challenges and there still seems to be few limits to his ambitions. In 2005, he was taking helicopter lessons and was rumoured to be looking around Scotland because he wanted to follow Roman Abramovich and buy the ultimate rich man's toy, a football club, in time for the start of the 2006–07 season. And none of his friends imagined that these would be his last big challenges or that any ambitions were off limits for the future.

'What would you like to come back as in your next life?' a reporter asked him recently.

'Prime Minister,' he replied, without a moment's hesitation.

We have been warned.